STRANGERS IN A STRANGE LAND

Vol. II Escape to Neutrality

By Hans-Heiri Stapfer/Gino Künzle

squadron/signal publications

A B-17 Flying Fortress is escorted to a landing field by a Swiss Air Force Morane MS-406 fighter while a P-51B Mustang flies overhead. The P-51B was formerly operated by the 4th Fighter Group before it diverted to Switzerland. The Swiss repainted it in Swiss markings and test flew the aircraft on a number of occasions.

ISBN 0-89747-278-0

If you have any photographs of the aircraft, armor, soldiers or ships of any nation, particularly wartime snapshots, why not share them with us and help make Squadron/Signal's books all the more interesting and complete in the future. Any photograph sent to us will be copied and the original returned. The donor will be fully credited for any photos used. Please send them to:

Squadron/Signal Publications, Inc.
1115 Crowley Drive.
Carrollton, TX 75011-5010.

Acknowledgements

The authors would like to thank everyone who supplied them with information and photographs for this book. There are far too many people and space limitations do not allow us to mention them all. We would like to thank all of the former internees who provided us with background information; the Swiss Federal Archives in Berne, in particular Monsieur Gauye and Herr Tschabolt; and Karl Hänggi who provided us with rare photographs and spent endless hours in his darkroom. Additionally, Franz Schraner, Dr. G. von Meiss and Peter Schneider provided valuable data and Herr Bernhard and Herr Küng of the Swiss Air Force Museum provided us with information from their files. We also would like to thank Mr. Klossner of the Swiss Federal Office of Military Airdromes for his friendly support.

In the United States of America, the National Archives and the Albert F. Simpson Historical Center provided us with information from the American side. Various Group Historians and Group contacts in 8th and 15th Air Force Associations helped us locating former internees. The Swiss Internees Association Inc. provided a great deal of assistance. The authors, sincerely hope that the U.S. Government will soon approve POW status for all internees. Last but not least, we would like to thank Squadron/Signal's tireless editor, Nicholas J. Waters III, for editing our poor English into American-ese.

Foreword

It is a little known fact that during the Second World War over 160 American aircraft sought refuge in neutral Switzerland. Rumors spread that most of these airmen had defected to Switzerland because they had enough of the war and wanted to spend the rest of the war in safety. In fact, the contrary is true. After over ten years of research, the authors feel that only about five to ten percent of the crews deliberately came to Switzerland. Additionally, a large number of American airmen escaped from Swiss Internee camps, making their way back to England or to Italy. Of the 1,740 internees and evadees, 947 tried to escape; of these, 184 attempts failed and the men were put into the tough Wauwilermoos prison camp.

Dedication

To the members of the Swiss Internees Association Inc. and to all American airmen interned in Switzerland during the Second World War — especially the sixty-one fliers who lost their lives in Switzerland.

B-17s and B-24s on the ramp at Dübendorf airfield near Zurich during the Winter of 1944/45. A total of 166 American aircraft sought refuge in Switzerland during the Second World War. (Swissair Archive)

Introduction

Switzerland is a Federal Republic consisting of twenty-five cantons (similar to the States of the U.S.) bordered by France, Germany, Austria and Italy. German is the dominant language in nineteen cantons, while French, Italian and Roman are spoken in the remaining cantons (Roman or "Romansh" is a language spoken in southeastern Switzerland).

Switzerland's 135 year-old policy of international impartiality and neutrality was maintained more in the letter than in the spirit of the law during the early years of the war. Despite, or perhaps because of, her neutrality, Switzerland had a difficult time during the Second World War. In 1940 Hitler took France in the notorious Blitzkrieg, completely surrounding Switzerland by Axis Forces. As a result, the Swiss were cut off from the United States and England. The Swiss claimed that they were willing to sell goods and weapons to both sides, although that became a little difficult as the Nazis cut off any avenue of export to the Allies. So for all intents and purposes, Germany and Switzerland became economic allies.

Switzerland, nevertheless, played an important part during the conflict and were able to act for the warring powers in matters relating to prisoners of war. All International Red Cross delegates who visited and reported on POW camps and conveyed complaints to the various governments were Swiss. Switzerland also accorded asylum to refugees, escaped prisoners of war from Axis camps, civilians and Jewish refugees. The number of refugees rose to 11,000 by May of 1945 and providing housing and food presented a considerable problem to the small Swiss nation.

At the beginning of the war, the Swiss Air Forces were underequipped and, apart from the Messerschmitt Bf 109E, most fighters were far below the latest standard. The numerically most important fighter in Swiss service was the Morane Saulnier MS-406 which was license manufactured in Switzerland. During May of 1940, the Swiss purchased an additional fifty Bf 109E-3 fighters from Germany.

By the end of 1939 there were 143 overflights of Swiss airspace by foreign aircraft. Neither Swiss fighters or anti-aircraft (AA) batteries

This Mosquito PR IV of the No 1 PRU based at Benson, Oxfordshire became the first Allied aircraft to land in Switzerland during the war. The aircraft had engine trouble on the way back from Venice and landed at Bern-Belp on 24 August 1942. The aircraft was tested at the Test and Research Center at Emmen near Lucerne. (F & W Emmen via Karl Steiner)

were brought into action however, since these border violations had taken place primarily at night or during adverse weather conditions.

On 21 April 1940, the first foreign aircraft landed in Switzerland: a Luftwaffe Dornier Do-17Z-3 of KG 2. The crew mistook Basel-Birsfelden airfield for a German field and landed. The aircraft and crew were interned by the Swiss. Later, due to pressure from Germany, both the crew and aircraft were returned to Germany.

Until the summer of 1942, all landings and/or crashes of foreign aircraft on Swiss soil were made by Axis aircraft. A number of Luftwaffe Bf 110 and He 111s were shot down by Swiss fighters and a number of Luftwaffe training aircraft landed in error in Switzerland.

In August of 1942, the first Allied aircraft came down in Switzerland and the circumstances of the landing were typical of most landings by Allied aircraft. While most Axis aircraft landed in Switzerland due to navigational error or because they were shot down by Swiss fighters, most Allied aircraft sought refuge in Switzerland because they were unable to return to their home base due to mechanical failure, battle damage or a lack of fuel.

The first landing of an Allied aircraft involved a Mosquito PR IV of No 1 PRU based at Benson, Oxfordshire, England. The pilot, G.R. Wooll, and navigator, SGT J. Fielden, were briefed for a reconnaissance flight to Venice on 24 August 1942. On the return leg, an engine overheated, forcing the crew to land at Bern-Belp airfield, near Berne, the Swiss capital. The crew attempted to destroy the Mosquito but they failed and the aircraft saw service with the Swiss Air Force. Both Wooll and Fielden were later exchanged for two Germans and one Italian and were back in England by late 1942.

The first American airmen to arrive in Switzerland did not land; they walked in. They had been shot down over Europe, were kept safe by the French underground and subsequently were guided to Switzerland. These men who escaped from the enemy, sought safety

The Messerschmitt Bf 109E-3 was the most advanced fighter in the Swiss Air Force. The BF 109E-3 (J-328) in the foreground nosed over on landing at Buochs airfield on 10 March 1941, but was subsequently repaired and returned to service. (Martin Kyburz)

Numerically, the most important fighter in Swiss service was the Morane Saulnier MS 406. This French design was license built in Switzerland as D-3800. J-32 was an MS 406 and carries the roundel style national wing markings in use during the early stages of the war. (Fotohaus Wiesner)

3

in Switzerland and walked unarmed into the country, were considered evadees rather than internees. According to a law which probably goes back to medieval times, evadees are entitled to sanctuary and are treated like tourists — perfectly free to leave. These evadees were kept in different camps from internees who arrived in Switzerland by air.

All airmen who either landed or parachuted onto Swiss soil were called internees. Basically, this meant that they were Prisoners of War in a neutral country, kept under guard at one place. The living standards of internees in Switzerland, however, were much better than those of POWs in Germany. Internees and evadees created their own meaning of Swiss neutrality. The Swiss were working for the Germans six days a week and praying for the Allies on the seventh.

That judgment is considerably harsher than the facts warranted. Despite the very questionable sympathies of some members of the Swiss government and of many industrialists and bankers, there was no mistaking the sentiments of the average Swiss. Probably some ninety percent of the Swiss people were openly pro-Allied.

13 August 1943

As time approached for the invasion of Sicily, the 9th Bomber Command was reinforced by B-24 Liberators from the 8th Air Force in England. Three bomb groups, the 44th, 93rd and 389th, were sent to North Africa during late June 1943.

These Groups were also involved in Operation TIDAL WAVE, the bombing of the oil refineries at Ploesti, Rumania on 1 August 1943. Upon return from Ploesti, the 9th Bomber Command was alerted for Operation JUGGLER. JUGGLER was a key allied plan to halt Luftwaffe fighter expansion in the west by striking coordinated blows at the German factories producing fighter aircraft. Two such targets were the Messerschmitt works at Regensburg in Bavaria and Wiener Neustadt near Vienna, Austria. As planned, JUGGLER was to employ 8th Air Force units against Regensburg, while the 9th attacked Wiener Neustadt from North Africa. The dual mission had been scheduled for 7 August 1943. Weather conditions, however, grounded the 8th Air Force in England. In the event, it was decided to forego the coordinated attack and let either force attack its targets at the first opportunity.

The 9th Air Force scheduled its attack for 13 August 1943. At 0700, 114 B-24s took off from their bases near Benghazi, Libya for the 1,200 mile flight to Austria. Each aircraft carried two extra bomb bay tanks, but even this extra fuel would be sufficient only to bring them back to bases in Tunisia. The raid into the heart of Germany was a complete tactical surprise and only two B-24 Liberators were lost.

One of these was a B-24D-75-CO of the 93rd Bomb Group named *Death Dealer*. It was flown by 1LT Alva Jack Geron and 2LT Russel P. Liscomb. Lt. Geron had been on the Ploesti raid flying that same aircraft. His original crew was incomplete since S/SGT Paul P. Daugherty had been killed over Ploesti and replaced by SGT Chaz L. Roberts and radio operator T/SGT Donald J. Grimes was on loan from the 329th Bomb Squadron. The other crew members were: bombardier 2LT Daniel R.E. Todd; navigator 2LT Robert V. Simpson; gunners SGT Richard G. Ryan, T/SGT David L. Wightman, S/SGT Gumecindo J. Frausto; and engineer S/SGT Thomas M. Osbsorn.

Alva Geron recalls the mission:

> *Our number three engine lost oil pressure and we feathered it before we reached the target. Over the target the number two engine sustained flak damage and we were no longer able to maintain altitude. We then took up a heading that we thought would take us to Switzerland. We flew through mountains, avoiding those peaks that were higher than we were. We finally identified what we thought was Lake Constance and made a pass over the Lake.*

The first American aircraft to land in Switzerland was set on fire by its crew after landing at Thurau near the city of Wil. The B-24D-75-CO (42-40611) had taken part in a raid on the Messerschmitt factory at Wiener Neustadt and was piloted by 1LT Alva J. Geron. (Hugo Landolt)

Swiss Air Force officers and enlisted men inspect the tail of the B-24D-75-CO Liberator. This was the first time the Swiss obtained information and actual hardware from an American four engined bomber. (Weltwoche Bilderarchiv)

1LT Alva Jack Geron and his crew pose in front of their aircraft 'Death Dealer'. They flew the Liberator from England to North Africa and then finally to Switzerland. (Alva Jack Geron)

Radio operator Donald J. Grimes told about the landing in Switzerland:

> We were in the back of the aircraft and were prepared to bailout on a signal from the pilot — but we never got the signal and suddenly we found we were too low to jump. There was nothing to do but ride it in. Luckily we had a few seconds to brace ourselves before the crash landing.

After the aircraft made a successful wheels down landing, some of the crew set the *Death Dealer* on fire, a common practice if an aircraft landed on non-allied territory. As the bomber circled over Eastern Switzerland a *Fliegeralarm* (Air Raid Alert) was given for the area. The alert was cancelled shortly after the Liberator landed at Thurau, near Wil at 1620 (Swiss time).

Donald Grimes recalled:

> While the plane was burning, Ryan and I had moved off some distance — probably 200 meters or so and were watching it when an older man came up to us. He was smoking a long curved pipe and looked like my vague idea of what a Swiss was supposed to look like. I said "Switzerland" and he said "Ja." This was the first time I knew of where we were!

Alva Geron told of their stay in Switzerland:

> We were escorted to the nearby town and questioned. The American Military Legation in Bern was notified and CAPT Free came to see us the next day. We were taken to Bern and then to Macolin where we were quartered until we were moved to Adelboden.

A few days later, specialists from Dübendorf Air Base began to dismantle the wreckage of the B-24 for examination. The parts were carried by trucks to the Wil railway station, then taken by train to Dübendorf. The remains of *Death Dealer* were stored in hangars at Kloten and scrapped during late 1945.

Alva Jack Geron was designated for exchange along with six other interned Americans for a number of German aviators. The Americans were sent to Spain and returned to the U.S. via Gibraltar and England. Ryan made an unsuccessful escape attempt from Adelboden and was taken to the Swiss prison camp of Wauwielermoos. He escaped again and crossed the border into France where he was caught in civilian clothes and shot by the Nazis. Donald Grimes worked at the American Legation in Bern, Robert V. Simpson attended the University of Geneva and Robert E. Todd worked for the American Red Cross in Geneva.

BATTLE QUEEN - Peg Of My Heart belly landed at Utzenstorf on 17 August. The individual aircraft letter "S" was carried only on the fin and the national insignia had a Red outline. (Karl Hänggi)

17 August 1943

Four days after the 9th Bomber Command launched their attack against the Wiener Neustadt Messerschmitt Works, the 8th Air Force sent the 4th Bomb Wing on a mission to the Regensburg Messerschmitt Factory as part of Operation JUGGLER. Simultaneously, the 1st Bomb Wing attacked the ball bearing works at Schweinnfurt in Bavaria. This second part of Operation JUGGLER would bring another two American bombers to Switzerland.

The mission plan called for the 4th Bomb Wing B-17s to continue south after hitting the target and, after crossing the Alps, Italy and the Mediterranean, land in North Africa. The force was faced with heavy fighter opposition and as the day ended, twenty-four 4th Bomb Wing B-17s and over 200 airmen were reported as missing in action.

Among these aircraft was a B-17F-85-BO (serial 42-30080) known as *High Life*, a combat veteran of the 100th Bomb Group with twelve missions over Germany. *High Life* was flown by Donald K. Oakes and his copilot, Joseph C. Harper. Their bombardier on this mission was Lloyd A. Hammarlund.

Jim Scott, the radio operator recalled naming the Flying Fortress:

> Our magnificent new Boeing B-17F was christened *High Life* while the crew was undergoing final overseas training at Wendover, Utah. We had High Life Beer and the Miller beer logo along with the pretty girl sitting on a half moon painted on the nose of our Fortress.

Jim Scott recalls the fighting over Germany:

> The enemy fighters swarmed on us about the time we crossed into Germany. The fighters came at us like jackals. I felt like an old man whose nerves had become petrified. During the attack, *High Life* suffered severe damage to the number two engine and received a direct hit on the number three engine from a Messerschmitt Bf 109 fighter. With two engines dead and one propeller windmilling our effective power was far below normal. *High Life* began to drop behind and in an effort to stay with the formation, Don Oakes told the bombardier to drop the bomb load. The bombs were jettisoned in a forest near Heilbronn, Germany. Even with the bomb load gone, our Fortress could not catch up with the formation and Oakes decided to pull away.

HIGH LIFE was the first B-17 to land in Switzerland. The Swiss lifted the bomber back on its wheels after its belly landing for further investigation. The ball turret and rear escape hatch are missing and the number three engine has been feathered. (Fotohaus Wiesner)

This B-17F-60-DL (42-3434) flown by 1LT Arthur F. Glasier was nicknamed *SO WHAT?* and was the first Flying Fortress to land intact in Switzerland. It was common practice to remove the guns before putting the aircraft into storage at Dübendorf. (H.J. Dubler)

6 September 1943

The 8th Air Force mission to Stuttgart on 6 September 1943 encountered a number of problems. Heavy clouds over the target prevented precision bombing, on the return leg a number of bombers ran out of fuel and some forty-five bombers were lost — and not a single bomb hit the primary target! Since Stuttgart is located fairly close to the Swiss border, a number of B-17s headed for neutral Switzerland; however, only four actually reached Switzerland safely and a fifth ditched in Lake Constance.

The first aircraft, *SO WHAT?*, of the 305th Bomb Group entered Swiss airspace shortly before 1030. The aircraft was flown by 1LT Arthur Franklyn Glasier and 2LT David John Engler. Engler had recently arrived in England on 1 September and the Stuttgart raid was his first mission. The crew of the B-17F-60-DL (42-3434) was faced with a lack of fuel and decided to go to Switzerland. They landed their virtually undamaged aircraft at Dübendorf Air Base. According to two Swiss interrogation officers, the morale of the crew from *SO WHAT?* was extremely low and one expressed the conclusion that this crew probably came to Switzerland deliberately.

RAUNCHY, a B-17F-85-BO (serial 42-30057) of the 100th Bomb Group was the assigned aircraft of 1LT Sam R. Turner and his crew. They had already flown some fifteen missions, but for the Stuttgart mission, the tail gunner S/SGT Norman F. Brett was replaced by SGT James E. Speakman. The bombardier, 2LT Vance R. Boswell recalls the mission:

> *Everything went well until we came off the target, then we were hit by fighters. I was hit in the left shoulder. Another burst hit the oxygen supply and another the instrument panel. Since there was no oxygen, we had to leave the formation.*

The 20MM shells struck the ball turret, killing S/SGT Joseph F. Moloney, as navigator 2LT Morris Weinberg discovered when he checked the turret.

BATTLE QUEEN - Peg Of My Heart rests on a flat car of the Swiss Federal Railways at Utzenstorf prior to shipment to Dübendorf for further investigation. All of the guns were removed prior to loading on the railway car. (Swiss Federal Railways)

> *The pilot ordered the crew to prepare to bailout. But before he made the final decision and rang the bailout alarm, our navigator Hiram E. Harris advised Oakes that Switzerland was only about thirty to forty minutes away. Deciding that we should make a run for Switzerland, Oakes swung High Life on the course that Harris had plotted.*
>
> *Our crippled Fortress was now down to about ten thousand feet as we sighted Lake Constance in the distance. We continued to lose altitude as we neared the lake. Suddenly a barrage of flak erupted around us. Luckily our Fortress was not hit and no one in the crew was hurt. We made it safely across the lake without further incident. The pilots looked for a flat piece of land and spotted an open field empty, except for a farmer. The landing gear would not go down so we cranked the wheels down manually only to discover that a tire had been ruined by flak. Hastily we cranked the wheels up again and assumed our crash landing positions. I prayed and silently cursed the Germans as our Fortress was making the approach for a crash landing. When the pilots brought High Life in for a wheels-up landing, there was a terrifying shock from the initial impact, together with the sound of tearing metal. As soon as the aircraft came to a halt, we scrambled out of the various exits.*
>
> *Swiss soldiers, in full battle dress and armed with rifles, appeared and surrounded us. The Swiss officer in charge told us in flawless English, "For you, the war is over. You are in Switzerland!"*

High Life was the first B-17 Flying Fortress to land in Switzerland and the bomber, which had belly landed at Dübendorf Air Base, was closely examined by the Swiss Air Force. It was decided to make the aircraft airworthy, but the plan was subsequently abandoned as flyable B-17s arrived in Switzerland. *High Life* was then dismantled and taken to Kloten for storage.

A second 4th Bomb Wing Fortress also sought refuge in Switzerland. *BATTLE QUEEN - Peg of My Heart* was a brand new B-17F-95-BO (serial 42-30315) assigned to the 390th Bomb Group. Flown by Stephen P. Rapport and Elmer R. Holloway, the Fortress had two engines shot out by German fighters. *BATTLE QUEEN* dropped out of formation and the crew decided to fly to Switzerland.

The crew found a large meadow suitable for landing just east of Berne. The belly landing at Uzenstorf damaged the fuselage and bent all four propellers. Shortly after the landing, a girl approached the crew and informed them that they were in Switzerland. For this reason, they did not set fire to the Fortress. The tail gunner, S/SGT Ricardo Robledo, had been hurt over Germany and was taken to a hospital.

Specialists from Dübendorf Air Base dismantled the aircraft and it was shipped by rail to Dübendorf for further examination. Two of the .50 caliber machine guns were given to the Federal Weapons Factory for examination.

RAUNCHY, the B-17F (42-30057) that 1LT Sam R. Turner ditched in Lake Constance, was later raised from the bottom of the lake and taken to Romanshorn where the body of the dead ball turret gunner SGT Joseph F. Moloney was discovered still in the turret. (Fotohaus Wiesner)

Vance Boswell told of the flight to Switzerland:

The fighters came on us like a bunch of bees. Sam Turner and Bill Freund did a great job of flying but we did not have a chance. The Messerschmit Bf 110s kept coming in and later the crew said they shot down six fighters. We were on one engine as we flew over Friedrichshafen at 300 feet, then out over the lake. Sam did some great flying. He had no flaps, no air speed indicator, nothing but guess and by golly. The landing on the water was perfect — the B-17 broke apart in the middle but we all got out. The Swiss came out by boat and took us to land. The Germans also came out, but the Swiss would not give us up. Thank God for that!

Pilot Sam Turner was slightly wounded in the chest by a shell fragment. He was exchanged for Germans during March of 1944. Vance Boswell was more severely wounded and lost the use of his left arm and the sight in his left eye. He was in the hospital for seven months. As the crew was interned at Adelboden, they named the hotel where they lived *Camp Moloney* and this name was officially adopted.

On 20 September 1943, the Swiss began to raise the Fortress from the bottom of Lake Constance where it sat in some 230 feet of water. On 16 October 1943, they finally succeeded and removed the dead turret gunner who was buried in the cemetery at Bag Ragaz.

Another 305th Bomb Group aircraft that ran into trouble was *Madame Betterfly* a B-17F-27-BO (41-24592). The Fortress was flown by 2LT Floyd E. McSpadden and his copilot 2LT Jack S. Noce. The navigator, 2LT Daniel G. Boone recalls the landing:

Our forced landing in Switzerland was a result of a shortage of fuel. Our number four tank fuel gauge was flashing red when we peeled off and headed for Switzerland. A Swiss fighter guided us to Dübendorf. No one was injured in the landing.

Copilot Jack Noce added:

We were housed in Swiss Army barracks for two days where we were questioned by Swiss Army officers.

Impatient Virgin II, a B-17F-105-BO (serial 42-30478), became the only 4th Bomb Wing Fortress to reach Swiss soil safely. It was one of twenty-four B-17s of the 388th BG from Knettishall which took off at 0547 not knowing that this would be the most disastrous mission flown by the 388th BG. Eleven aircraft failed to return. The formation was met by the strongest fighter opposition encountered to date with about 150 enemy aircraft, consisting mainly of Focke Wulf 190s, Messerschmitt Bf 109s and 110s. The fighter attacks were very intense from the Initial Point (IP) to the target.

Impatient Virgin II was flown by 1LT William P. Beecham and his copilot F/O Barlow Dean Brown. The rest of the crew were new and this was their first mission as a crew.

During the fighter attacks, the Fortress fell out of formation and headed for Switzerland where they landed safely. The B-17 had no signs of damage and still had some 750 gallons of gas in the tanks.

This B-17F-105-BO (42-30478) was flown by 1LT William P. Beecham and was on its second mission. *Impatient Virgin II* left the Boeing assembly lines on 7 June 1943 and arrived in Switzerland on 17 August. The Swiss found no damage to the aircraft and 750 gallons of fuel remained in the tanks. (Fotohaus Wiesner)

During the flight to Switzerland, the crew destroyed all documents and items of important equipment.

The crew gave no information to the Swiss interrogation officer, since they feared that any information given to the Swiss would be immediately forwarded to the Germans.

The brand new B-17F was taken into service with the Swiss Air Force and a few days after the landing, it took off for a test flight repainted with Swiss markings. At least four test and demonstration flights were conducted at Dübendorf before the aircraft was transferred to the Test and Experimental Center at Emmen where the aircraft remained for the rest of the war. On 3 September 1945, COL Karl Högger and Engineer Wachtmeister (SGT) Franz Schraner flew the Fortress to Dübendorf, where it was flown back to Burtonwood two days later by an American crew.

The last landing that day was by a B-17F-25-VE (serial 42-5841) of the 306th Bomb Group aircraft named *Est Nulla Via In Via Virtuti* (Latin for "There is no way impossible to courage"). The saying had been applied by the pilot, 1LT Martin Andrews, an experienced pilot with a well trained crew. Navigator Charles G. Bowers recalled the mission:

As a sign of impending trouble, our chief engineer and ball turret gunner were seriously injured in a jeep accident on the runway going to our plane. We received two replacements from our squadron and took off. Once in formation and crossing the French coast, we experienced the usual anti-aircraft fire and a few German fighters, both of which intensified as we approached the target area. During the next wave of fighter attacks, our inboard engines were hit after which we could no longer maintain the formation's altitude or speed. Our pilot, Martin Andrews, feathered the props on the bad engines as we turned away from our Group about twenty minutes from the target. We dropped our bombs in what we thought to be an uninhabited woods hoping to avoid killing any civilians. Since I had only my small silk "Escape" map of southwest Germany and northern Italy, I gave the pilot a "rough" heading to Switzerland. We decided to land unarmed and throw overboard all ammunition, machine guns and strategic radio equipment. With two engines out, we had great difficulty avoiding the Swiss Alps.

1LT Martin Andrews landed his B-17F-25-VE (42-5841) at Magadino in Southern Switzerland where *Est Nulla Via In Via Virtuti* was placed under guard by Swiss soldiers. The individual aircraft letter had not been applied to the vertical fin and the national insignia was outlined in Red. (Martin Kyburz)

Impatient Virgin II on the ramp at Dübendorf during trials by the Swiss Air Force. The U.S. national insignia, group markings and aircraft serial number were overpainted and replaced with Swiss markings. At least four flights were conducted and recorded before the B-17F was transferred to Emmen Test and Research Center. (Weltwoche Bilderarchiv)

MADAME BETTERFLY had served for about a year with the 305th BG. On her last mission, the B-17F-27-BO (41-24592) had been flown by 2LT Floyd E. McSpadden. All guns were removed from the ship during its storage at Dübendorf. (Weltwoche Bilderarchiv)

The bomber circled for a while over the Swiss-Italian border area. At the same time, CAPT Von Meiss, a flight instructor at the only Italian language Swiss Air Force pilot's school at Magadino airfield was returning with his pupils from a training flight in their MS 406s. Shortly after he landed, a mechanic jumped on his wing and told him that an American bomber was circling over the border looking for a place to land. The Captain took off and flew alongside the B-17 signaling him to follow.

Charles G. Bowers remembered the landing:

Actually we were guided to a small landing strip by a friendly Swiss fighter. As he waved us down, our waist gunner mistook the Swiss emblem for the Red Cross symbol, shouting "we're ok!" After a rugged landing we were "captured" at Magadino by the Swiss Army and taken to the local Commandant's office. We had planned to burn the aircraft on landing and each crewman was to throw an incendiary bomb into a specific area of the plane. I tore up all my navigation maps and opened my parachute in the nose area. Fortunately none of the bombs went off - otherwise with the plane's nearly empty gas tanks, it would have surely exploded!

The crew was sent to Macolin and subsequently transferred to Adelboden. The B-17F was transferred to the Test and Experimental Center at Emmen on 22 October 1943. On 5 September 1945 the aircraft was handed over to American authorities and flown to England on 15 September 1945.

1 October 1943

1 October 1943 became a historic day for the B-17s of the 12th Air Force. It was the first time that units of the North African based 12th AF would bomb targets in Germany. The target was the Messerschmitt works at Augsburg, a round trip of some 1,800 miles. Also in the attacking force were B-17s of the 99th Bomb Group, which was based at Oudna in Tunisia.

Twenty-two aircraft took off at 0811 led by COL Upthegrove and, of these, seven returned early because of mechanical troubles. The attacking force failed to reach the target because of a solid undercast and they turned back some sixty miles south of the target area. Flak encountered enroute to the target was generally heavy to moderate and fairly accurate. COL Upthegrove recalls the mission.

I think we we were third or fourth in the Wing and as we reached the Alps, we passed a Group or two returning and we wondered why they were aborting. North of the Alps, all of Southern Germany appeared to be covered with a thick overcast. We decided to abort and had turned back when thirty or so

Yellow nosed Me-109s appeared and began frontal attacks in groups of four to six abreast. I thought I had an idea of how to combat this and as they wheeled around to start their next firing run, I would dive down about 200 feet. They flew right through our formation and after they passed, I would climb back 200 feet. We repeated this over and over until the fighters used up their ammunition and withdrew. We continued and the navigator tried to get a position report, but the overcast prevailed until we reached the Alps.

These first formations jettisoned their bombs mainly through the overcast, or on targets of opportunity, such as the small town of Feldkirch close to the Swiss border where some 168 persons died. Almost all of these formations violated the Swiss airspace on the return flight and, on several occasions, bombs were dropped on Eastern Switzerland. Fortunately, these did not cause serious damage.

Air raid alarms were sounded in Switzerland as the first wave of bombers crossed the border. Flak Det 21 (Anti-aircraft Detachment Number 21) under the command of COL G.F. Ruegg was placed on alert. The unit was equipped with 75MM Vickers anti-aircraft guns and was the first heavy AA-gun unit established in the Swiss Army. It was based at Ragaz-Buel, only three miles from the Swiss-Austrian border. The unit had fired, on several occasions, at foreign aircraft which violated Swiss airspace.

The 99th Bomb Group, one of the last elements leaving Germany, crossed into Switzerland and COL Ruegg recalled:

The group was flying in three moderately open wedges in line over the Sargans basin. There, the group was once again attacked by German fighters and the battle was observed by Anti-Aircraft Detachment Number 92. The group did not change formation during the aerial fighting and flew, with some loss of altitude, directly towards our anti-aircraft position. I could see that the second or third plane had a contrail behind one of the engines on the left wing, yet there was no fire. German fighters were no longer in the area and I decided to fire at the group as they passed overhead. The lead aircraft of the left squadron was sighted by the fire-control director while another director was sighted on the aircraft on the leader's left wing. We opened fire about thirty seconds after the flight passed directly overhead, firing in the direction of Landquart.

The second aircraft of the left unit was shot down by our AA fire and plunged towards the earth with long flames trailing from the engines. After a few seconds, the Flying Fortress exploded. Two men bailed out of the plane, their parachutes opening immediately (COL Ruegg did not see the third man that also bailed out safely).

The B-17 that COL Ruegg shot down was a B-17F-85-BO (serial 42-30126), named *Sugarfoot*. It was flown by 1LT Burton C. English and his copilot 2LT Donald M. Prentice. The rest of the crew included: navigator Stanley L. Finseth, bombardier 2LT Irving B. Patten, engineer T/SGT Peter B. Malchiodi, radio operator T/SGT Joseph R. Carroll, assistant radio operator S/SGT Charles R. Burgett, tail gunner S/Sgt Elmer D. Wheadon, left waist gunner Marion Dale Pratt and right waist gunner Norris W. King.

The officers of *Sugarfoot* were photographed at Oudna the day before they were killed in action over Switzerland (1 October 1943). From left to right: bombardier 1LT Irving B. Patten, LT George Coen (not on the mission and now president of the 99th BG Association), co-pilot 2LT Donald M. Prentice, pilot 1LT Burton C. English and navigator 2LT Stanley Finseth. (George F. Coen)

The wreckage of *Sugarfoot* was taken to Dübendorf, where the B-17F wreckage was reassembled for further investigation and technical study. (Swiss Federal Archives)

Marion Pratt recalls the mission:

We were flying on the extreme left of the formation and enemy fighters singled out our plane for concentrated attacks. On the first attack, our ship was hit by cannon and machine gun fire that caused a lot of damage to the front of the plane. A minute or so later, the fighters attacked again, with one diving at us from above. This time we were hit by everything they had. The front, waist and tail were filled with bullets and exploding cannon shells.

Suddenly, the plane gave a buck and I was thrown to the floor. This may have saved my life for just as I went down a burst of fire went through the waist and back towards the tail. During this attack, I believe that most, if not all, of the five men in the front of the aircraft were killed. I am also convinced that this burst killed Elmer Wheadon, our tail gunner. The B-17 was on fire but I did not know it at the time. We had also crossed the Swiss border and the Swiss were shooting at us as well. I found this out later from a Swiss officer.

Just as I was trying to get on my feet again, our plane exploded. I can not say for sure whether it was the gasoline or the oxygen supply that exploded. When the Fort exploded, it nosed forward and started toward the ground at a tremendous rate of speed. The plane was going down so fast that Norris King and I were floating against the top of the plane. I was quite sure at that time that it was all over for us.

Suddenly what was left of the plane, or at least the part that King and I were in, leveled off a little and we fell back on the floor. Everything was a turning and twisting dream. My mind began to clear a little and I began to wonder if I could get out.

Hauptmann C.F. Ruegg (left) and Hauptmann Hühnerwadel of the Swiss Military Police talk with two survivors from *Sugarfoot*, waist gunner S/Sgt Marion Dale Pratt (middle) and radio operator Joseph R. Carroll at the funeral of their unfortunate comrades at Bad Ragaz. (Oberst G. F. Ruegg)

On 5 October 1943, a funeral was held at Bad Ragaz for fourteen unfortunate American airmen who had been killed over Switzerland. Each coffin was covered with an American flag and among the guests were GEN Legge (U.S. Army) along with the Polish and British military attaches. (Jim Scott)

Though the haze, I saw the waist window with the gun torn off. I gathered all my strength and rolled myself toward the window. I reached it and placing my foot on the edge of the window and shoved myself out into space.

Marion Pratt, Norris King and Joseph Carroll were the only survivors from the B-17.

The other badly shot up aircraft, a B-17F-30-VE (serial 42-5856) continued in the formation for a short time before crashing at Alvaneu. The crew of this ship included: pilot 1LT William J. Cantwell, copilot 2LT Marvin R. Boydston, navigator 2LT W.H. Breslin, bombardier 2LT Norton L. Marks, engineer SGT Bruce S. Rowen, radio operator T/SGT Jesse G. Maddox and gunners SGTs Saturnino Chavez, Murray R. Phillips, Gordon T. Schenkelberger and K.A. Higinbotham. Shortly before takeoff, an aerial photographer, S/SGT Herbert McArdell, had also joined the crew for the Augsburg mission.

LT William Cantwell recalls the mission:

We were flying on the far right of the group in the "Tail End Charlie" position. The aircraft on my left was hit in the nose and cockpit area from a Bf 109 and I saw it go straight down but I was rather busy at the time. That aircraft and mine were behind the main formation. I had one engine out and was unable to feather the propeller. My aircraft was hit repeatedly by machine gun and perhaps cannon fire from the attacking fighters. Engines number one, two and three were out and I had no control of the power setting on number four. It could only be controlled with the ignition switch. All intercom and radio communications equipment was shot out and I could not talk to anyone on board except the copilot. The bomb bay doors would not function, so I pulled the manual release for the doors and the bombs. If any were released, I did not know it. My altitude at this time was about 18,500 feet and we were going down rapidly. I signaled the men in the nose area to jump. The top turret gunner Bruce Rowen and LT Boydston went. I had previously flipped the bailout alarm switch, and since I could not control the aircraft any longer, I abandoned it via the nose hatch behind the others.

Only the men in the nose section of the aircraft survived. William Cantwell, Marvin Boydston, W.H. Breslin, Norton Marks and Bruce Rowen were subsequently picked up in the mountains and guided down by Swiss Army soldiers.

On Tuesday, 5 October 1943 the bodies of the men killed in the crashed aircraft at Ragaz and Alvaneu, as well as turret gunner Moloney from the bomber salvaged from Lake Constance were buried in the cemetery at Bad Ragaz with full military honors.

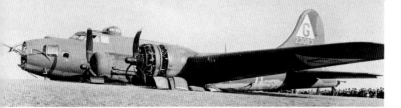

This B-17F-120-BO (42-30831) named *LAZY BABY* made a belly landing at Reinach-Aesch. The navigator's compartment was hit, killing the navigator 2LT Donald T. Rowley. The 305th BG applied the Group identification marking on the undersurface of the starboard wing. (Kantonspolizei Baselland)

14 October 1943

The second Schweinfurt mission was the most disastrous raid ever flown by the 305th Bomb Group based at Grafton Underwood, England. Of the sixteen B-17s that departed on the raid only three returned to England. Twelve ended up down in Germany, but one had a little more luck and reached Switzerland.

The aircraft was a B-17F-120-BO (serial 42-30831) flown by 2LT Edward W. Dienhart and copilot 2LT Brunson W. Bolin. The other crew members included navigator 2LT Donald T. Rowley, bombardier 2LT Carl A. Johnson, engineer T/SGT George H. Blaylock Jr., radio operator T/SGT Hurley D. Smith, ball turret gunner S/SGT Raymond C. Baus, right waist gunner S/SGT Christy Zullo, left waist gunner S/SGT Robert Cinibulk and tail gunner S/SGT Bernard Segal. The aircraft was called *Lazy Baby* although the name was not painted on the aircraft.

Gunner Christy Zullo recalls the Schweinfurt mission:

Our escort had just about reached their limit of travel and were getting ready to go back to their bases. They left us about five minutes from Frankfurt and there they were, Focke Wulfs by the dozens! They began their first pass at our formation and they were painted exactly like our escort ships. I could not tell they were German aircraft until I saw the flashes from their cannons.

I began firing and they just kept coming in, one right after another. I hardly knew which one to fire at, but I kept my gun going all the time. One Focke Wulf made an attack at the nose of our ship coming in from about eleven o'clock. He hit our waist, putting a rip in the floor right between my legs. It went through my boot and cut a nice slice in my heated flying suit, but did not reach my leg. It frightened me for a while, but when I saw that I was not bleeding, I went back to firing my gun. On their next pass at us, my oxygen system was shot out and my mask drew close to my face every time I took a breath. Everything began to get black and as I was falling to the floor, I managed to reach the walk around bottle. I plugged my mask into it and after taking a few heavy breaths, I began to feel alright. Another cannon shell hit in the waist, bursting over our heads. It put a few big dents in the right waist gunner's helmet and a few holes in the back of my flak suit. At that instant a piece of flak hit the nose of our ship, breaking the plexiglas and hitting our bombardier Carl A. Johnson and the navigator Donald T. Rowley.

There was no use trying to keep in formation because our ship was full of holes and three men were very seriously injured. The pilot rang the alarm bell to warn us to bailout, but back in the waist, I had my headset pulled out and I did not hear him. The copilot Brunson W. Bolin and engineer George H. Blaylock had already bailed out and the pilot put our plane in a dive. I was thrown against the right side of the waist and managed to get my flak suit off and attach my parachute to its harness. We threw out the waist door and got ready to jump when the ship began to level out just above the trees. There were no fighters around us, so I went up to the radio room and began to dress some of the radio operator's wounds, he had been hit by shell fragments from a 20MM shell which had burst in the radio room. We traveled south for about an hour hoping to find Switzerland and finally we saw the Swiss flag waving beneath us. There was no airfield nearby and our gas was just about finished, so we made a wheels up landing in a farmer's field. LT Dienhart made a perfect landing and saved our lives.

Edward W. Dienhard landed his B-17 at Reinach-Aesch near Basle. The badly wounded navigator Donald T. Rowley was immediately taken to the hospital at Basel, but all efforts to save him failed and he died the following night. He was subsequently buried at the Cemetery of Hörnli in Basle.

The Flying Fortress was dismantled and taken to Kloten where it was stored for the remainder of the war.

The Winter Months

Only three American aircraft came down in Switzerland during January and February of 1944. By 1 January 1944, a total of eighty-six American airmen were interned at various places in Switzerland. Some Swiss officials wanted to put them to work on road gangs but American officials protested, pointing out that all the airmen were either officers or noncoms and, under the Geneva Convention, not liable for forced labor. Protests were also made that the proposed barracks for the Americans were inadequate, lacking both ample living space and recreational facilities — important considerations for combat men suddenly thrown into a long period of enforced idleness.

The first landing during 1944 involved a B-24H-2-FO (serial 42-7519) of the 93rd Bomb Group. The unit suffered three losses on the 7 January 1944 raid to Ludwigshafen. After bombing the target, the Liberator experienced superchargers trouble on three engines, which prevented it from maintaining formation. The crew, under 1LT David M. Richardson decided to divert to Switzerland. For a while the ship circled over Berne before it was guided by a flight of fourteen Morane fighters to Dübendorf airbase where it made a safe landing. No damage to the Liberator was discovered and there was still enough fuel for about three hours of flight.

The combined plan for 25 February 1944 called for some 400 15th Air Force "heavies" to depart from their Italian bases for the Messerschmitt works at Regensburg. The 8th Air Force dispatched 754 bombers against Regensburg, Augsburg, Stuttgart and Fürth. The Fifteenth lost thirty-nine bombers, while the Eighth lost thirty-one. One ship from each of these forces landed in Switzerland.

The Italian based B-24 Liberators of the 47th Wing were led by the 450th Bomb Group from Manduria. They came under heavy and violent fighter attack all the way to and from the target, with the Luftwaffe claiming four 450th BG Liberators. One bomber that ran into trouble was *Liberal Lady*, a B-24H-10-FO (serial 42-52148). Under constant attack, the crew had to feather two engines and despite the damage, decided to fly to Switzerland. Albert L. Thompson, the engineer recalls:

I was the flight engineer and radio operator on this flight since we were one man short for this mission. Our original aircraft, Geanne, was lost during another mission and the 25 February mission was the first time we flew the Liberal Lady.

1LT David M. Richardson's B-24H-2-FO (42-7519) diverted to Switzerland after suffering supercharger failure on three engines. The Liberator's nose art had not been finished by the artist before the B-24 made its last flight, landing at Dübendorf. (Fotohaus Wiesner)

DOTTIE G a B-17G-10-DL (42-37755) of the 92nd BG was the first G-model to land in Switzerland. It was jacked up by the Swiss after making a belly landing so they could study the nose turret. The soft ground and snow prevented the chin turret from being smashed. There were ten mission symbols painted on the nose. (Peter Schneider)

16 March 1944

On 16 March 1944, the 1st and 3rd Air Divisions bombed targets in Bavaria and the 2nd Air Division attacked Friedrichshafen on Lake Constance. In all 740 heavy bombers were dispatched and twenty-three failed to return.

The first aircraft that came down in Switzerland was *Mount'n Ride*, a B-17G-20-BO (serial 42-31585) of the 91st Bomb Group. The B-17 suffered damage to number two and three engines and the pilots 1LT Robert C. Mersereau and 1LT Doyle Bradford, feathered the props and took up a course for Switzerland landing at Dübendorf airfield.

The 385th Bomb Group had been briefed to bomb the Messerschmitt factory at Augsburg. About one hour from the target, eight to ten Messerschmitt Bf 109s attacked the formation. The B-17G-30-DL (serial 42-38160) flown by 1LT Robert W. Meyer was hit, knocking out the number four engine and slightly wounding T/Sgt Carl J. Larsen. At 1135 hours the ship turned south towards Switzerland.

Tail Gunner S/Sgt. Jarrell F. Legg stated in a report written shortly after the war:

> At the Swiss border, we were picked up by an escort of Swiss fighters. They were very similar to the German 109s so they lowered their wheels and flaps and began to fire flares. We acknowledged with a flare and they came in and tried to lead us to a landing field, but we were unable to stay in the air since we were constantly losing altitude. At about 500 feet, the pilot gave the order for us to bailout.

As the crew left the aircraft over Baar on the Lake of Zug some over-enthusiastic Swiss began shooting at the Americans, thinking they were paratroopers invading their country. At least three shots were fired by Army riflemen.

Unfortunately, the navigator, 2LT Robert L. Williams', parachute did not open properly and he hit the ground at Neugasse in Baar. He was immediately taken to the hospital at Baar, but died a short time later. Carl L. Larsen and ball turret gunner S/SGT Charles W. Page also received medical help from the Swiss.

The pilot had remained aboard, circling over the lake in preparation for a water landing. He made his approach in direction of the small town of Zug. After landing, the aircraft remained afloat for about five minutes before it sank about 1,500 feet from the shore. Two Swiss rescued the pilot from the lake and took him to the police station in Zug. During the Summer of 1952, Martin Schaffner managed to lift the Fortress from the bottom of Lake Zug. After being repaired, the name *Lonesome Polecat* was added to the nose and the Flying Fortress was exhibited throughout Switzerland before it was finally scrapped at St. Moritz during the early 1970s.

MOUNT'N RIDE, a B-17G-20-BO (42-31585), was painted by the famous artist Tony Starcer. USAAF ground crewmen and Swiss air mechanics posed with the bomber during the Summer of 1945 while it was being prepared to return to England. (A. Kistler)

Shortly after reaching Swiss airspace, the Liberator was intercepted and escorted by five Morane of *Fliegerkompanie* 12 (Aircraft Company 12). The crew bailed out of the aircraft at intervals near the city of Wil and the pilotless aircraft crashed at Braunberg.

The crew was picked up by Swiss soldiers shortly after landing. After being interrogated, the nine men, under the command of 2LT William R. Cranston, were sent to Adelboden. Albert Thompson later was assigned to the U.S. Foreign Office in Zurich.

The 92nd Bomb Group of the 8th Air Force was briefed to attack the ball bearing works at Stuttgart. The unit suffered two losses and one of missing aircraft, *Dottie G*, successfully made it to Switzerland. This B-17G-10-DL (serial 42-37755) had been assigned to the 325th Squadron on 16 September 1943. It had survived eleven mission and was flown by on this mission by 2LT Clifford P. Beach and his co-pilot F/O Homer L. Ford.

At 1418, while still in the target area, the Fortress was attacked by rocket firing Bf 110s. With the number three engine hit, the bomber dropped out of formation and headed for Switzerland. While in combat with the Bf 110s, bombardier PVT William A. Lenovich shot down one of the fighters (while the bombardier on a B-17 was usually an officer, Lenovich was a PVT).

Exactly one hour after the aircraft was hit over Germany, Clifford P. Beach crash landed the *Dottie G* at Dübendorf airfield.

The Swiss air force had a particular interest in the aircraft since it was the first B-17G with a chin-turret (all other B-17s previously downed were the earlier F variants). The Fortress was hoisted up on its wheels and the chin turret was closely examined. The Swiss were particularly interested in the angle of fire of the turret. This examination helped to develop new attack tactics against the bomber, just in case an American aircraft would not willingly follow the escorting Swiss aircraft.

Big Noise, a B-24D-120-CO (42-40969) was a veteran of the famous Ploesti low level raid. 1LT Richard J. Pettit landed the Liberator at Dübendorf where the Swiss found no damage and enough fuel in the tanks for a return to England. (Fotohaus Wiesner)

This B-17G-10-BO (42-31329) carried the 95th BG's Command Pilot, MAJ Noel Strader, who was riding in the copilot's seat beside the pilot, 1LT James Reed. The Fortress became quite a local attraction for the people at Oberriet-Kriessern. (Kantonspolizei St. Gallen)

Big Noise, a B-24D-20-CO (serial 42-40969) was one of the only losses for the 93rd Bomb Group on 16 March. The Liberator was flown by 1LT Richard Pettit and his copilot 2LT Humphrey Elliott. Shortly before take off, Pettit was forced to loan his assigned navigator to the squadron lead Liberator. As a result, the B-24 flew the mission without a navigator. After the bombing run, the aircraft left the formation and flew to Dübendorf, where it landed. The Swiss noted that the aircraft was undamaged and there was about 1,058 gallons of fuel remaining in the fuel tanks.

A B-17G-10-BO (serial 42-31329) of the 95th Bomb Group was selected to carry the Command Pilot and Observer, MAJ Noel Strader, who was leading the Augsburg force to the target. He was riding in the copilot's seat beside the aircraft's pilot, 1LT James Reed. The tail gunner had also been replaced by 2LT David Harte, who was acting as an additional observer.

The navigator 2LT Murray Ball recalls:

We received a direct hit on the number three engine which immediately caught fire and all attempts to feather the propeller failed. The vibration was so severe that the plane had to be slowed to about 115 miles per hour. We were prepared to bailout over Germany but were reluctant to do so with Switzerland so close so we immediately headed for Switzerland with one or two German fighters making passes on us.

Our gunners had considerable experience and were quite good. I don't know what happened, but after a while we were alone. Soon the vibration in the engine stopped, we guessed the crankshaft broke. What a sight — Lake Constance. After passing over the Lake, I told the pilot, Jim Reed, that we were in Switzerland and to land in a particular field that I pointed out. Those not needed for the actual landing assembled in the radio room, dislodged the hatch cover and prepared for a crash landing. In circling the field to make the final approach we passed over Austria. Jim Reed charged back to the radio room and stated he saw a Swastika on a roof below the plane. I told him to land in the field that I had pointed out earlier. He said I had better be right. That faithful old B-17 landed like a pair of skis, wheels up.

Shortly after the landing at Oberriet-Kriessern, the Swiss Army came to collect the crew. The bomber was dismantled and taken by train to Kloten for further storage.

Another aircraft which was badly damaged by the Germans was a B-17G-30-DL (serial 42-38195) from the 385th Bomb Group. The crew bailed out over Ragaz; however, the command pilot, Bernhard Wasserman, and navigator, Robert Fillmann, landed in German territory. The rest of the crew, under the command of 1LT Vincent P. McLaughlin safely reached Swiss soil.

The pilotless Fortress crashed in a wooded area close to the small town of Wildhaus, only 1,500 feet away from the local church. The next day, a salvage team from Dübendorf began to dismantle the aircraft which, because of its location, was quite difficult. Finally, on 24 March 1944, three railroad cars of wreckage were sent to Dübendorf.

Another victim of the air defenses over Friedrichshafen was a B-24J-70-CO (serial 42-100116) flown by 2LT Secar J. Harris. The rest of the crew included: copilot 2LT Stewart J. Van Der Veen, navigator 2LT Julius Rosenfeld, bombardier 2LT John E. Gilmore, engineer S/SGT Joseph E. Helms, radio operator S/SGT Clyde A. Forrester and gunners SGTs Marshall M. Ward, Leask W. Hermann, Wayne G. Moeller and John M. O'Neill.

Left waist gunner, Leask Hermann recalled the flight:

Our plane lost one engine over France and another was damaged over the target so our officers decided our plane could not make it back to England and tried to make it to Switzerland. Our navigator did not have the correct maps and we were lost. Finally it was decided to bailout. I was the fifth man to leave the plane. I landed between the Rhine river and a canal near the Swiss town of Au. The navigator, LT Rosenfeld, was also fortunate and landed in Switzerland. The eight other crew members landed in Austria and were POWs for the rest of the war.

The pilotless aircraft (serial 42-100116) of the 93rd Bomb Group circled over Austria and Germany before crashing near the Swiss town of Schlattingen. According to Swiss civilians who witnessed the crash, the number one engine was burning before the crash.

The only loss for the 389th Bomb Group based at Hethel, England, was a B-24J-90-CO (serial 42-100332) named *Galloping Katie* which successfully escaped to Switzerland. The Liberator, flown by 2LT August M. Snyder and his copilot 2LT Sheldon Bray, lost two engines on the way to Friedrichshafen. The number three engine lost oil pressure and the propeller on number four had to be feathered. About twenty-five miles southeast of Lake Constance the pilot knew that he could not stay with the formation on the trip home. After the bomb run, he turned toward Switzerland. Over Dübendorf he was met by Swiss fighters which guided them down. The aircraft was scrapped after the war; however, the two good engines were used on other B-24s which were in a better condition.

2LT August M. Snyder took this B-24J-90-CO (42-100332) to Switzerland during mid-March of 1944 with a feathered propeller on number four engine. Despite the icy conditions, *GALLOPING KATIE* made a safe landing. (Fotohaus Wiesner)

18 March 1944

Two days after their first attack on Southern Germany and Bavaria, the 8th Air Force returned to hit industrial targets and airfields. Once again, the 2nd Air Division (B-24s) was briefed to attack Friedrichshafen, while the 1st and 3rd Air Divisions attacked Munich, Oberpfaffenhofen, Lechfeld, Landsberg, and Memmingen. A total of 738 bombers took off from England and as the day ended, forty-three were reported as missing in action. Of these, sixteen had landed in Switzerland.

First arrival in Switzerland was *Pistol Packin Mama* a B-24H-1-FO (serial 42-7513) of the 445th Bomb Group. The ship was flown by 1LT Jan H. Sefton and 2LT Stephen M. Skvarentina. Right waist gunner S/SGT John C. Miner tells about the mission:

> *We had just crossed the German border when our number two engine malfunctioned and had to be shut down and the propeller feathered. We were able to maintain our group position on three engines and were approximately half an hour from our target, when we passed over a barrage of flak and lost our number three engine. We were unable to hold altitude on two engines and we dropped out of formation. Losing altitude, we had only one viable option — to head for Switzerland.*

The aircraft was intercepted and escorted by Swiss fighters to Dübendorf. On final approach the Liberator's landing gear caught and destroyed the high voltage cable of the Swiss Federal Railway. Luckily, *Pistol Packin Mama* was able to continue to a safe landing.

1LT William A. Kala's *Lil Gypsy*, a B-24H-1-CF (serial 41-29127) of the 392d Bomb Group, was off to the left of the main group formation for approximately twenty minutes prior to the target. After salvoing its bombs the aircraft went under the formation to the right, heading towards Switzerland. With no oil pressure on number one engine and the propeller feathered, Kala landed the ship at Dübendorf.

While on the way to Oberpfaffenhofen, 2LT William V. La Seur's B-17G-30-BO (serial 42-31871) lost number one and two engines due to anti-aircraft fire. He pulled the Fortress out of the 384th BG formation and headed for Switzerland. The ship was intercepted and escorted

This B-24H-1-CF (42-29127) Liberator originally deployed overseas with the 446th BG before being transferred to the 392nd BG. 1LT William A. Kala landed *Lil Gypsy* at Dübendorf with number one engine out and the propeller feathered. (Fotohaus Wiesner)

by Swiss fighters to Dübendorf, but La Seur's landing was too fast. After touchdown, he had no alternative but to retract the landing gear to slow the aircraft which was headed towards houses located at the end of the runway. The plane came to a stop, but the underside was damaged and the propeller blades were bent.

1LT Gordon L. Capps' B-17G-15-VE (serial 42-97515)S was hit by flak over Lechfeld where he lost one engine followed by a second a few minutes later. The Fortress, which had been assigned to the 92nd Bomb Group, left the formation at 1440 hours. With two propellers feathered the ship was escorted to Dübendorf airfield by Swiss fighters. After overshooting the runway, the pilot retracted the undercarriage of his B-17, damaging the engines and fuselage. Ball turret gunner CPL George E. Jones later escaped from Switzerland and attempted to join up with allied troops in Italy. Unfortunately, he was captured by the Germans and spent the rest of the war as a POW.

Happy Go Lucky, a B-24H-2-FO (serial 42-7625) of the 446th BG, flown by 1LT Edward Jennings, lost oil pressure on the number two engine due to a mechanical failure. Flak over Friedrichshafen damaged the number four engine and the prop had to be feathered. On two engines, 1LT Jennings left the formation and crossed Lake Constance. Swiss fighters intercepted the Liberator only a few miles before the ship reached Dübendorf and escorted the B-24 in for landing. The crew tried to burn the B-24, but quick action by Swiss soldiers saved the *Happy Go Lucky* from destruction.

1LT George W. Mears was leading the low squadron of the 351st Bomb Group in *Superball*, a B-17G-15-DL (serial 42-37825), against Landsberg/Lech airfield. T/SGT Richard D. Hobt recalled:

> *Almost immediately after the bomb run, Fw 190s attacked us from the six o'clock position level passing through our formation. They turned and made a level head on pass from 12 o'clock. The three aircraft in the lead element were hit by a heavy concentration of machine gun and cannon fire and were, I think, heavily damaged. We were struck in the nose, a 20MM shell exploding in the navigator's compartment and another shell exploded at the base of the pilot's control column. A large*

SACK ARTISTS, a B-24J-65-CO (42-100073) on the ramp at the 44th BG's home base at Shipdham, England, carried command pilot CAPT Robert L. Cardenas on his last mission. The Liberator crashed at Fehraltdorf after the crew bailed out. (Will Lundy)

2LT William V. LaSeur's B-17 suffered engine damage on the number one and two engines. The B-17G-30-BO (42-31871) overshot the runway and retracted the landing gear, damaging the wing and propeller. (Karl Hänggi)

hole was blown in the left side of the fuselage just below the top turret. Numbers one and two engines were shot out and an oil fire started in number three. The pilot was stunned by the exploding shell and lost control of the aircraft. We went into a steep dive, passing under our left wingman just as he exploded. We fell from 18,000 feet to about 5,000 feet before the copilot and the pilot regained control. After we assessed our damage and loss of fuel we knew that a return to England was out of the question, so we headed east towards the Swiss border. As we crossed the border, we were intercepted by four Morane fighters. Due to our damage, we felt we could only attempt one pass. We came in downwind and on contact with the ground, the landing gear collapsed.

1LT Roger C. Smith flew a B-17G-10-DL (serial 42-37793) named *Spirit Of Winsome Winn II* of the 384th Bomb Group. The ship was badly damaged by flak and landed in Switzerland. LT Smith, in a report written in October of 1944 stated:

Prior to the landing, the supercharger was inoperative, the number one engine was on fire and windmilling, the number three engine had been hit by flak and was windmilling and the oil line had been also hit by flak. The plane was on fire when the landing was made.

The Fortress almost overshot the small grass airstrip at Altenrhein on the Swiss side of Lake Constance and the pilots were forced to retract the undercarriage. The B-17 was subsequently dismantled and taken by train to Kloten Air Depot for storage.

1LT Walter T. Hebron left the 392nd Bomb Group's formation at 1514 flying a B-24H-10-DT (serial 41-28692). The ship had received three hits in the tail section and the tail turret was inoperative due to a cut hydraulic line. Although the damage was bad, it was a lack of fuel that forced the crew to set course for Switzerland. Morane fighters intercepted and escorted the Liberator to Dübendorf.

Only the tail section of this B-24J-70-CO (42-100112) Liberator was undamaged after the B-24 crashed near Dietschwil. 1LT Hollis R. Nichols and his crew bailed out and the pilotless bomber crashed a short time later. (Karl Hanggi)

Shortly before reaching the target area, 1LT G.T. Haffermahl, flying a B-24J-105-CO (serial 42-109826) of the 392nd BG, panicked from flak and enemy fighters and pushed the bailout alarm. He was the first to jump and not realizing the actual situation on board, three gunners followed him out the bomb bay.

Over the target the B-24 was hit by flak in the nose and in one engine. The copilot 2LT Donald H. MacMullen managed to extinguish the fire in the engine by diving the aircraft, but exploding ammunition in the nose badly wounded the bombardier 1LT Samuel B. Poppel. Fortunately, the navigator, 2LT Kenneth C. Parks, succeeded in extinguishing the fire in the nose. By then the ship had lost the formation and there was no hope of reaching England. The copilot and navigator decided to fly to Switzerland, where a landing was made at Diessenhofen. The crew set the aircraft on fire and the burnt remains of the Liberator were taken to Kloten on 22 March 1944.

The B-24J-85-CO (serial 42-100284) which carried the 715th Squadron commanding officer, CAPT Jack P. Edwards, was the only loss for the 448th Bomb Group. The aircraft was heavily damaged by anti-aircraft fire and left the formation with a severe fuel leak heading for Swiss territory. Swiss fighters escorted the ship to Dübendorf where a Swiss ground crew counted over 100 cannon and flak holes in the Liberator. S/SGT Robert Miltner, the badly wounded gunner, was taken to a hospital at Zürich, but later died of his wounds. The Swiss Air Force began to dismantle the aircraft on 9 June 1944 for storage at Kloten.

The 44th Bomb Group lost eight aircraft that day, but six of these actually escaped the Germans by flying to Switzerland. The 44th had to make two passes over the target, and on the second pass the flak was able to concentrate their fire against the only group over Friedrichshafen. This second pass resulted in damage to most of the Group's aircraft and six of them were so badly damaged that a return to Shipdham was out of question.

2LT Eugene W. Dyer's B-24J-105-CO (42-109800) made a successful landing at a Swiss base. Swiss ground crewmen found some 675 gallons of fuel in the tanks and no real damage to the Liberator. (Karl Hänggi)

2LT Winston C. Irwin diverted to Switzerland in this B-24H-15-CF (41-29431) with a damaged number four engine. When *SHOO SHOO BABY* landed, there was only 108 gallons of fuel left in the tanks. (Karl Hänggi)

1LT Robert R. Lucas' B-24J-100-CO (42-100400) suffered flak damage to three of its four engines. When he landed at Dübendorf the nose-wheel of the Liberator collapsed. (Karl Hänggi)

Sack Artists, a B-24J-65-CO (serial 42-100073), carried the group command pilot, Robert L. Cardenas. It was on fire and so badly damaged that the entire crew had to bailout over Fehraltdorf near Dübendorf air base. The entire crew safely reached Swiss soil, but the copilot 1LT Jack R. Tinney was wounded in the face.

1LT Hollis R. Nicols and his crew left their aircraft, a B-24J-70-CO (serial 42-100112) shortly after they crossed the Swiss border and the pilotless bomber crashed at Dietschwil.

The first 44th BG aircraft to come down safely at Dübendorf was a B-24H-15-CF (serial 41-29431) named *Shoo Shoo Baby*. It was piloted by 2LT Winston C. Irwin. The copilot 2LT Uriah G. Hartman recalled:

> *There were direct hits in the number four engine, tail turret and on the turbos of numbers two and three engines. The hydraulic system was out and the fuel lines had been cut. On entering Swiss airspace, Messerschmitt Bf 109 fighters approached us on the starboard wing and I instructed the gunners to hold their fire. We landed on a taxiway, since the airfield had other damaged bombers on the runways.*

2LT Eugene N. Dyer's B-24J-105-CO (serial 42-109800) was the next to land at Dübendorf. There was virtually no damage to the aircraft and there was some 675 gallons of fuel left in the tanks.

1LT George D. Telford and his crew were intercepted by Swiss fighters and escorted to Dübendorf. No damage was recorded by the Swiss Air Force personnel, but there was only about 540 gallons of fuel left on board the B-24H-2-FO (serial 42-7618).

Just after bombs away, at approximately 1446, 1LT Robert R. Lucas left formation under control and flew across Lake Constance. The B-24J-100-CO (42-100400) was damaged in the number one, three and four engines, as well as being badly hit in the fuselage. During the landing, the nosewheel collapsed and damaged the nose of the aircraft. On 15 June 1944 Swiss salvage crews began to dismantle the aircraft for storage at Kloten.

The record of sixteen aircraft down in Switzerland on a single day was never repeated during the war. Additionally, by the end of the day the 44th BG had more aircraft interned in Switzerland than any other USAAF organization.

SPIRIT OF WINSOME WINN II, was damaged upon landing at Altenrhein. The B-17G-10-DL (42-37793) was dismantled and taken by train to Dübendorf. Such an event was always a big attraction for the local Swiss people, since aircraft of this size were uncommon in Switzerland. (Mattias Weichelt)

Super Ball, a B-17G-15-DL (42-37825), made it to Dübendorf with the number one and two engines out and the propellers feathered. 1LT George W. Mears flew the Fortress on its last mission. (Karl Hanggi)

This B-17G-15-VE (42-97515) bellied in at the airfield boundary and was dismantled. A FBW truck tows the bomber's fuselage to a hangar at Kloten. Modified Swiss Federal Railways flat cars were normally used for such transports. (Fotohaus Wiesner)

(Above)
1LT Edward Jennings landed his B-24H-2-FO (42-7625) at Dübendorf with the propeller on the number four engine feathered and the number two engine losing oil. The Liberator overran the runway and the right main landing gear sank into the soft ground. (Karl Hänggi)

(Below)
A lack of fuel forced 1LT Walter T. Hebron and his crew to land this B-24H-10-DT Liberator (41-28692) at Dübendorf. The White of the fuselage markings were overpainted with Gray to tone down the markings. (Karl Hänggi)

(Above)
1LT Jan H. Sefton's B-24 H-1-FO (42-7513) had the propeller on the number one engine feathered and the number two engine had lost a lot of oil. On final approach to Dübendorf, the ship's landing gear cut the high voltage lead cable of the Swiss Federal Railways. (Karl Hänggi)

(Below)
Command pilot CAPT Jack P. Edwards landed this badly leaking B-24J-85-CO (42-100284) at Dübendorf. Accurate German anti-aircraft fire peppered the Liberator with more than 100 holes and seriously wounded S/SGT Robert Miltner who later died in the hospital. (Karl Hänggi)

16

13 April 1944

April Fools Day of 1944 saw a deterioration in the diplomatic relationship between Switzerland and the United States when Liberators of the 392nd and 44th Bomb Groups bombed Schaffhausen, the only large Swiss city north of the Rhine river. In the accidental attack, some forty civilians were killed, thirty-three houses were totally destroyed and a further seventeen were heavily damaged. This tragic error was hard to understand for many Swiss and rumors spread that the Americans deliberately bombed the city because there were a number of companies located here that were working for the Germans.

The next time American bombers sought refuge in Switzerland, some aircraft were deliberately shot up by Swiss anti-aircraft units. It is unknown, however, if these incidents were meant as a retaliation for the bombing or not. On 13 April 1944, the 8th Air Force dispatched 626 bombers to Schweinfurt, Oberpfaffenhofen, Lechfeld and Augsburg. Thirty-eight aircraft were reported as missing in action, but of these, thirteen flew to safety in Switzerland.

The first aircraft down was a B-17G-35-BO (serial 42-32073) of the 96th Bomb Group which had a "Cheyenne" tail turret, a modification new to the Swiss. The bomber was flown by 2LT William C. Potter and 2LT Donald W. Malloy. The bombardier, 2LT James V. Calire recalled:

We left the formation before the approach to the target; we had no damage but we had lost fuel. Regarding the decision to come to Switzerland, the pilot had the final word. The landing was no problem - but rough!

Group operations officer CAPT Lawrence F. McGuire and CAPT Oliver F. Keller taxi in their badly damaged B-17G-40-BO (42-97064). There were twenty-seven flak holes in the aircraft. The Olive Drab cheek gun framing was a replacement borrowed from another Flying Fortress. (Karl Hänggi)

The new Cheyenne turret was studied by Swiss officers and during late May the American markings were replaced by Swiss crosses. The first flight was conducted on 1 June 1944 under the control of COL Högger and Wachtmeister Schraner. The flight lasted some thirty-five minutes and at least four other flights were recorded. These flights were conducted to develop the best attack angles against the new Cheyenne turret.

2LT H.L. Kreuzer and his copilot Lawrence P. Koenig flew their badly damaged B-17G-5-BO (serial 42-31184) to Switzerland. The crew bailed out of the 447th Bomb Group Fortress over Dübendorf and the pilotless aircraft headed southeasterly towards Rapperswil on Lake Zurich. Swiss fighters shot down the bomber which crashed about 2.5 miles from Siebnen on Lake Obersee. The wreckage was later salvaged by the Swiss Air Force and taken to Kloten for storage.

The next aircraft to land at Dübendorf was from the 447th BG which had been briefed to attack the Messerschmitt factory at Augsburg. This B-17 was flown by 2LT Joseph R. Thornbury and his copilot F/O Albert E. Cowey. Enemy fire had damaged the number two engine and the crew left the formation and headed for Switzerland, where a Morane escort guided the bomber to Dübendorf.

A 390th Bomb Group B-17G-25-BO (serial 42-31691) flown by 1LT Donald L. Cooper and his copilot 1LT Robert Cockrum, headed for Switzerland because enemy fire had slightly damaged two engines and ruptured the fuel tanks. Some of the crew knew that there was different treatment for an internee (a flier who came directly from combat to a neutral country) and an evadee (someone who walked unarmed into a neutral country after being shot down over enemy territory).

2LT H.L. Kreuzer and crew bailed out over the Dübendorf area and Swiss fighters shot down the pilotless B-17G-5-BO (42-31184). The bomber caught fire and crashed near Siebnen on Lake Obersee. Only the tail of the bomber survived the crash. (Karl Hänggi)

2LT Donald G. Jorgensen had only 130 gallons of fuel remaining in the tanks of his B-17G-30-DL (42-38196) Flying Fortress when he touched down at Dübendorf. The Swiss found over thirty five-holes in the aircraft from enemy fire. (Karl Hänggi)

With the number three engine feathered, 2LT William C. Potter taxied his B-17G-35-BO (42-32073) in after landing at Dübendorf at 1355. The ship left the Boeing Seattle assembly lines on 21 January 1944 and was the first B-17G with a "Cheyenne" tail gun position to land in Switzerland. (Karl Hänggi)

Potter's B-17G-35-BO (42-32073) after the American markings were replaced by Swiss insignia crosses. The group markings, a "C" in a square was faintly visible on the fin. The first test flight was conducted on 1 June 1944 by Oberst Hogger and Oberleutnant Heitmaneck. (Franz Wegmann)

Trying to obtain "evadee treatment," the crew worked out a special plan.

After crossing the Swiss border, they circled over Dübendorf, then landed in a large meadow at Langenzinggen. The Fortress bent the propellers during the belly landing, but otherwise the bomber received little new damage. When the aircraft came to a rest, the crew left the bomber and hid in a nearby forest.

2LT Robert J. Dooley taxis in his B-24H-1-DT (41-28629) at Dübendorf. F8-P was an one of the original inventory of the 453rd BG and deployed overseas with the Group. The number two engine was damaged and there were ten shell holes in the Liberator. (Karl Hänggi)

As the Swiss officers totalled the crews that had arrived that day, they found out that one crew was missing — that of aircraft 42-31691. After a couple of hours, Swiss soldiers found the crew in the forest. The crew stated that they just escaped from a German POW camp, crossed the Rhine river and were therefore evadees! For the surprised Swiss soldiers all this was very suspicious since the "evadees" still wore their flying clothes and were completely dry. They told the same story to Interrogation Officer CAPT Von Meiss repeatedly. They stated that they were not the crew of the Flying Fortress which landed only a few yards from the place where they were found! Finally the Swiss called an American official who came to Dübendorf and after a talk with the crew, advised Donald L. Cooper and his men to tell the Swiss the truth, which they did.

2LT Robert J. Dooley and his crew left the 453rd Bomb Group on the way to Oberpfaffenhofen near Lake Constance. The B-24H-1-DT (41-28629) suffered a failure of the oxygen system, shortage of fuel and a loss of oil in the number two engine. Near Zurich the plane was damaged by accurate Swiss anti-aircraft fire. Two of the crew bailed out and were picked up by the Swiss Army near Turbenthal. After landing at Dübendorf, the Swiss counted ten holes in the wings and fuselage of the B-24.

The heavy anti-aircraft fire over Augsburg badly shot up 2LT Raymond W. Gault's B-17G-30-BO (serial 42-31747). The number one engine had to be feathered and the number two fuel tank was steadily leaking fuel. Radio operator T/SGT Frank J. Bonz recalled:

We were to bomb at 20,000 feet and on arrival over the target, about 100 flak guns fired on our formation. In spite of the accurate flak, we dropped our load of forty-two 100 pound incendiaries. After the bombs were away, we were hit by flak. Three pieces of flak went through my radio room: two going through the radio table, missing me by an inch. We could not make it back to Bury St. Edmunds, so we headed for Switzerland. We were picked up by two Swiss fighters and escorted to a safe landing.

1LT Donald L. Cooper bellied in his B-17G-25-BO (42-31691) at Oberglatt. The 390th BG ship was dismantled and taken to Kloten for storage. All the Fort's guns except those in the top turret have already been removed. (H.J. Dubler)

2LT Gordon R. Wiren's B-17G-35-BO (42-31977) received hits in the fuel tanks leaving it short of fuel for the flight home. The chin turret has unusually long gun barrels on the two .50 caliber machine guns. There were some thirty holes found in the Flying Fortress. (Musee de l'Air)

The Swiss counted no less than thirty-four machine gun and four cannon holes in the badly damaged B-17G. On 24 May 1944, a Swiss salvage team began to dismantle the aircraft for storage at Kloten.

2LT Gordon R. Wiren's B-17G-35-BO (serial 42-31977) landed only three minutes after Gault's Fortress. The aircraft had a windmilling propeller on number four engine and a leaking fuel tank, caused by the accurate flak over Augsburg. As the bomber crossed the Swiss border, Swiss anti-aircraft hit the aircraft over the Winterthur area. 2LT Gordon Wiren; however, made a safe landing at Dübendorf. About thirty holes were found in the aircraft which was dismantled on 27 April 1944 for storage at Kloten.

2LT Doald G. Jorgensen and F/O James Sellar flew a B-17G-30-DL (serial 42-38196) to Augsburg and the aircraft became another victim of the heavy and accurate flak over the target. With holed fuel tanks, the ship headed for Switzerland. Shortly after crossing the border, Swiss guns fired on the aircraft and scored hits on the fuselage underside. Finally, Swiss fighters intercepted and guided the stricken bomber to Dübendorf where it landed with only forty minutes of fuel remaining. Some twenty-one bullet and fourteen shell holes were found in the aircraft.

1LT Rockford C. Griffith and his crew could be labelled as a hard luck crew. Out of their previous twenty missions they were damaged twelve times. And their hard luck continued on the way to Lechfeld. Radio operator S/SGT Forest S. Clark recalled:

We were apparently hit by anti-aircraft fire over the target and lost some fuel. Then we had to stop one engine and could not make it back to England. Rather than crash in Germany and be taken prisoner, we decided to try to land in Switzerland.

Shortly after the B-24J-90-CO (serial 42-100330) crossed the Swiss border anti-aircraft fire greeted the Liberator.

I fired off a lot of distress flares to let Swiss officials know we were in distress and wanted to land at Dübendorf. When we landed, I had to destroy the secret equipment for radar tracking and communications inside the plane. This was done by touching off an explosive charge. Swiss troops with machine guns surrounded us on the ground, but we were glad to be alive.

During the Augsburg raid, the 447th Bomb Group lost the leadship after the bomb run. The B-17G-40-BO (42-97064) ran into heavy and accurate AA fire which damaged the number four engine. The ship carried CAPT Lawrence F. McGuire as operations officer and was flown by CAPT Olivier F. Keller and 1LT John M. Hodges. Shortly after crossing the border, Swiss anti-aircraft fire hit the aircraft. The navigator 1LT William E. Bird was knocked from his seat and he injured his elbow. Ground crews counted no less than twenty shell holes in the aircraft.

B-17G-30-BO (serial 42-31866) was another 385th BG ship which did not make it back to Great Ashfield that day. The aircraft was flown by 2LT Harvey R. Downs and 2LT James R. Bigham. The waist gunner, S/SGT Raymond Koenig, told about the mission:

Accurate anti-aircraft fire damaged 2LT Raymond W. Gault's B-17G-30-BO (42-31747) Flying Fortress. The number one propeller had to be feathered and most of the instruments, including the fuel controls were out. (Karl Hänggi)

2LT Joseph Thornbury landed this B-17G-35-DL (42-107021) with the number two engine feathered at Dübendorf. Later the defective engine was replaced and all the guns were removed. (Fotohaus Wiesner)

This B-17G-30-BO (42-31866) was hit in the number three and four engines. In addition, some thirty-eight holes were found in the aircraft. The cheek gun positions were a modification to the B-17G flown by 2LT Harvey R. Downs. (Karl Hänggi)

The 13 April 1944 mission was my next to last mission, since I was supposed to fly 29 and this was my 28th. The crew I flew with was not my regular crew except for pilot, LT Downs, who was my regular copilot. Our regular crew, except for LT Downs, myself and the tail gunner, had finished their missions. Downs and I were interned, but the regular tail gunner was shot down with another crew and was in a POW camp in Germany. Over the target we were badly damaged by anti-aircraft fire and had to leave the formation. We had one engine out, one damaged and some of the controls were gone. The left waist gunner was wounded and we were in a bad shape.

While I was giving first aid to the wounded man, we were hit by two enemy fighters. They made one pass at us and finished another engine. We fired at them and one was smoking when they left. This damage killed any chance of reaching England so the pilot asked for a heading for Switzerland. Over Switzerland, we were picked up by two Swiss fighters and they guided us to an airport.

Rhapsody in Flak was a 95th Bomb Group B-17F-95-BO (serial 42-30233) flown by 2LT Harvey A. Johnson and F/O Clyde A. Northcott, Jr. Flak over the target knocked out the number two and four engines and the pilots decided to try for Switzerland. After crossing Lake Constance, they landed at Altenrhein airfield.

1LT Rockford Griffith diverted to Dübendorf with this B-24J-90-CO (42-100330). The number two engine was feathered and the number one engine was losing oil. The Liberator had been fitted with additional armor glass in the cockpit. (Karl Hänggi)

A Swiss built Saurer truck tows *RHAPSODY IN FLAK* out of the soft ground. 2LT Harvey A. Johnson's B-17F-95-BO (42-30233) sank into the soft ground after the landing at Altenrhein. Enemy fire had damaged the number two and four engines. (Karl Hänggi)

1LT Lesley E. Kring (front center) was the original pilot of *RHAPSODY IN FLAK*. The B-17F-95-BO (42-30233) took the crew on the Regensburg raid then to North Africa. At this time, the Fortress carried the old Group marking and the individual aircraft letter "X." (Lesley E. Kring)

After repairing the damage and replacing two engines, Oberst Karl Högger and Wachtmeister Franz Schraner ferried the bomber from Altenrhein to Dübendorf on 3 May 1944 where the aircraft remained for the rest of the war.

2LT Norman C. Flynn's B-24H-15-FO (42-52567) was the last aircraft to seek refuge in Switzerland that day. The 466th Group met accurate flak over the target and the number three engine was shot out just short of the target. The crew continued on and dropped their bomb load before peeling away for Switzerland. The badly damaged bomber crossed the border near Schaffhausen and was then escorted by Swiss fighters to Dübendorf. No less than forty holes were found by the Swiss ground crew in the wings and fuselage of the Liberator. One of the gunners, S/SGT James A. Gribble, managed to escape from Switzerland and was back at his home base by 20 September 1944.

2LT Norman C. Flynn landed his B-24H-15-FO (42-52567) Liberator with the number two engine feathered at Dübendorf. The lower portion of the rudder was covered in oil from the damaged engine. There were some forty shell holes found in the aircraft. (Karl Hänggi)

24 April 1944

2Lt Max E. Wilson's B-17G-25-BO (42-31632) hit a radio shack at Dübendorf airfield on landing. The individual aircraft letter and Group marking was carried on the tail. The rear escape hatch was missing. (Karl Hänggi)

On 24 April 1944, the 8th Air Force sent 754 bombers over the continent, with all three Air Divisions being briefed to bomb targets in Southern Germany and Bavaria. Forty aircraft would not return that day, but fourteen of them made it to Switzerland.

On the way to Oberpfaffenhofen, 1LT Thomas R. McClure's B-17G-30-DL (42-38204) was engaged by enemy fighters over Strassbourg. The fighters inflicted heavy damaged to the aircraft, setting the number three engine on fire and the propeller windmilling. A direct hit in the waist area seriously wounded one of the gunners and a cannon shell exploded only three feet behind the tail gunner, SGT George A. Senheiser, causing further damage. McClure and his co-pilot, 2LT John S. Putiri, jettisoned the bomb load and set course for Switzerland. They crossed the border near Basle and flew to Geneva, where they landed on the hard surfaced runway. The seriously wounded gunner was immediately taken to the hospital in Geneva. The Fortress remained in a hangar at Geneva until it was flown by Oberst Högger and Wachtmeister Schraner to Dübendorf on 13 July 1945. The aircraft was later scrapped.

2LT Max E. Wilson and his crew were on their forth mission in their B-17G-25-BO (serial 42-31632). The regular bombardier, 2LT George Prokopec was grounded due to a head cold and SGT John Dzedzy was assigned as bombadier for the flight. This was to be Dzedzy's twenty-fifth mission, ending his combat tour.

The tail gunner, S/SGT Ronald W. Grove recalled the flight:

On the way to the target, the number 4 engine was feathered due to an overheated cylinder. Flying on three engines, we still were able to stay in formation. As we approached the target, we

encountered enemy fighters and later, flak. A Focke Wulf Fw 190 blasted the number two engine loose in its nacelle and the loss of two engines forced us out of formation and we jettisoned the bomb load. Shortly thereafter, the number one engine began losing oil as a result of flak damage. With only the starboard inboard engine functioning, we began to lose altitude rapidly. Our pilot was preparing the crew for bailout when it was discovered that at least two parachutes had flak damage and were useless. The navigator 2LT Virgil Y. DeCamp, then began working up our location relative to the Swiss border.

The pilots had located an open field and planned to attempt a wheels down landing, figuring the ground would still be frozen. The remainder of the crew were in the radio room preparing for a crash landing. On touchdown, the main landing gear on the port side collapsed. The impact knocked the copilot, 2LT Kowalczyks' head against the armor plate and he suffered a concussion. The crew in the mid-section suffered various bumps, bruises and sprains. The aircraft went into a 90 degree port turn and headed uncontrollably toward a Swiss radio substation and tower. The radio shack was demolished as the B-17 crashed through it and the starboard wing root made contact with the radio station tower bringing the aircraft to a jarring halt.

The next Fortress to land in Switzerland that day was a B-17G of the 95th Bomb Group. The B-17G-35-BO (42-31993), named *GENRIL OOP* was flown by 2LT Edward G. Cunningham and had received flak damage in the tail shortly before reaching the target area. Over Friedrichshafen, the B-17 lost the number one engine and the number two engine was badly leaking oil. The crew pulled the bomber out of formation and sought refuge in Switzerland, where they safely landed at Dübendorf.

Still shaken, but safe, 1LT Thomas R. McClure's crew waits under guard by a Swiss Army Corporal. The crew was under constant fighter attack all the way to the target. (Karl Hänggi)

Swiss soldiers and police officers inspect the B-17G-30-DL (42-38204) stored in the hangar at Geneva-Cointrin airfield. For the Americans, Swiss uniforms and helmets appeared very similar to those of the German army. (Karl Hänggi)

1LT Roy A. McCallum suffered engine failure of the number four engine. Additionally the Fortress lacked sufficient fuel to return to base. His B-17G-45-BO (42-97138) had an Olive Drab nose hatch taken as a replacement from another ship. (Fotohaus Wiesner)

1LT William W. Parramore's B-17G-45-BO (42-97203) suffered severe damage to the nose section during its landing at Altenrhein. The Fortress was taken by road to its final storage place at Dübendorf. (Fotohaus Wiesner)

formation and sought refuge in Switzerland, where they safely landed at Dübendorf.

The Flying SAC, a B-24J-135-CO (42-110098) of the 448th Bomb Group was the only Liberator to come down in Switzerland that day. 1LT John A. McCune and his crew were briefed to attack Gablingen airfield in Bavaria. On the way to the target the number two engine overheated and lost oil. As a result the propeller was feathered. Increasing power on the remaining three engines resulted in a higher fuel consumption and north of Strasbourg, *The Flying SAC* left the formation and headed for Switzerland. The Liberator landed at Dübendorf with only 540 gallons of fuel left in the tanks.

On that same day a B-17G-30-BO (42-31921) of the 407th Bomb Squadron, 92nd Bomb Group met a tragic fate over Switzerland. The crew included the pilot, 2LT James E. King, copilot 2LT Myron P. Snapp, navigator F/O Ned E. Lewis, bombardier 1LT Martin J. Thomas, radio operator S/SGT Urvin J. Laperriere, engineer SGT Raymond H. Hardy, ball turret gunner SGT William H. Lowery, waist gunners SGTs Russell Harris and Felix J. Scefonas and tail gunner SGT Pasquale A. Calabrese.

The Fortress was shot up by enemy fighters and at least two engines were damaged. The bomber flew to Switzerland and circled over Dübendorf at 600 feet. Swiss civilians later reported that the number three and four engines were out and fuel was streaming

from the aircraft forming a white contrail. As the aircraft turned onto the final approach, it suddenly went into an uncontrolled dive and crashed at Baltenswil with no survivors. Funeral services were held for the crew on 27 April at the American cemetery at Münsingen.

2LT Irwin Schwedock was flying an early B-17G-5-BO (42-31172) that left the Boeing plant with the standard Olive Drab and Neutral Gray camouflage and without cheek guns. These were later added at a modification center and the paint was stripped to gain more speed. About an hour before the 306th Bomb Group reached their target at Oberpfaffenhofen, the low group was repeatedly attacked by German fighters. LT Schwedock's gunners claimed five enemy aircraft, but the B-17 lost the number two engine which could not be feathered. Due to the additional drag, the Fortress was left behind the formation. The crew jettisoned the bomb load and headed for Switzerland where they landed safely at Dübendorf.

2LT Virgil Ray Broyhill and his crew flew a B-17G-15-DL (42-37885) of the 384th BG named *Frostie*, although the name was never painted on the ship. Over the French coast, a flak shell exploded near the tail and slightly wounded the tail gunner, T/SGT James R. Robertson. Shortly before reaching the target, some forty Bf 109s jumped the formation and T/SGT Robertson shot one down. Heavy and accurate flak damaged the number one engine and the prop had to be feathered. The number four engine lost oil and the number two engine began to overheat. Broyhill dropped out of formation and flew to Switzerland. Shortly after they crossed the border, a Swiss anti-aircraft unit fired on them, but luckily they missed the Fortress.

1LT John A. McCune taxis in his B-24J-135-CO (42-110098) Liberator at Dübendorf airfield. The number two engine was feathered and the number three engine was shut down. Additional armor plates installed in the cockpit area cover part of the name *Flying SAC*. (Karl Hänggi)

Trailing contrails, B-17s from the 306th Bomb Group go through flak enroute to Berlin. The B-17G-20-BO (42-31539) in the foreground landed in Switzerland some weeks later. The Black smoke above the Fortress was caused by an exploding rocket fired by a German fighter. (USAF)

1LT Dale Ebert belly landed his B-17G-20-BO (42-31539) at Neftenbach, smashing the chin turret. The number four engine lost oil pressure and the number one engine was ripped from its mount. The crew jettisoned the ball turret before landing. (Fotohaus Wiesner)

1LT Roy A. McCallum and his crew were flying a B-17G-40-BO (42-97138) from the 94th Bomb Group when they ran into trouble two minutes short of the initial point. They left formation with the number two engine smoking. The bomber landed with number two and three propellers feathered, and only 486 gallons of fuel remaining on board.

1LT William W. Parramore's B-17G-45-BO (42-97203) was attacked half an hour before the target by enemy fighters, which scored hits on the number two engine which could not be feathered. Dispite the additional drag, Parramore managed to stay with the formation and bombed the target. Since one of the gunners was wounded and the stricken ship was losing the formation, 1LT Parramore decided to try for Switzerland. They landed at 1400 hours at Altenrhein where the Fortress nosed over, destroying the entire nose section. The copilot 2LT Oscar C. Sampson and the bombardier, 2LT John H. Garcia later made the first successful escape attempt from Switzerland. Both had previously tore down the Nazi flag from the German consul's office at Davos where all officers were interned. The Nazis protested and Swiss officials ordered that the two Americans be sent to a punishment camp, but friendly Swiss civilians helped them escape and they made their way into France with the help of the French underground.

SHOO SHOO BABY, a B-17G-25-BO (42-31669) of the 303rd Bomb Group was flown by 2LT Raymond Hoffmann and his co-pilot 1LT Robert W. Snyder. The navigator 1LT Samuel Minkowitz recalled the mission:

We lost one engine due to fighters before we got to the target. Over or near the target we were hit by flak which damaged a second engine, causing the prop to runaway. The prop could not be feathered and since we could not make it back to England, we headed for Switzerland where we landed at the airport at Zurich.

A B-17G-30-BO (42-31758) flown by CAPT John J. Stolz was hit by heavy and accurate flak, damaging the left wing. The number two

engine had to be feathered followed by the prop on the number three engine, and the Fortress from the 306th Bomb Group set course for Switzerland where they landed at Dübendorf. The aircraft was subsequently dismantled and taken to Kloten on 2 June 1944.

Another 306th Bomb Group aircraft which did not make it back to England was 1LT Dale Ebert's B-17G-20-BO (42-31539). Dale recalled the flight:

We flew our first mission on 24 December 1943 but were not assigned to Fortress 539 until late January of 1944. The Fortress was attacked by enemy fighters which knocked one engine out. At an altitude of 900 feet, we crossed Lake Constance and were shot up by Swiss anti-aircraft guns. We jettisoned the ball turret and the machine gun from the radio compartment. The pilots bellied in at Neftenbach and the tail broke away from the fuselage.

Little Chub, a B-17G-50-BO (42-102446) of the 384th BG, was attacked by German fighters over Stuttgart. The top turret gunner S/SGT Raymond A. Newall stated in a report written after the war:

When attacked by German fighters, we were hit in the nose by two cannon shells, and the bombardier, 2LT Jesse L. Greenbaum, who was on his first mission, was badly wounded being hit in the face.

The pilot, 1LT Everett L. Bailey and copilot, 2LT James E. Burry left the formation at 1405 at an altitude of 22,000 feet and headed for Switzerland. The rest of the crew included navigator 2LT Charles D. Wallach, radio operator S/SGT William J. Silag, ball turret gunner SGT Anthony T. Melazzi, tail gunner SGT Sidney Pratt, right waist gunner SGT Richard R. Hollingsworth and left waist gunner SGT Richard M. Sendlback (who had a broken a leg). He was been taken to the radio room, while the badly wounded bombardier Jesse L. Greenbaum was laid on the walkway between the copilot and pilot and given first aid by the crew.

2LT Irvin Schwedock flew this battered B-17G-5-BO (42-31172) Flying Fortress to Switzerland. The aircraft has a non-standard anti-glare panel and a B-17F style top turret. (Karl Hänggi)

CAPT John J. Stolz took his B-17G-30-BO (42-31758) to Switzerland after feathering the number two engine and finding that the number three engine could not be feathered and was windmilling. The port wing was heavily damaged by an explosive shell. (Karl Hänggi)

2LT Edward G. Cunningham landed his B-17G-35-BO (42-31993) with the number one engine feathered and the bomb bay doors stuck open. The rear emergency hatch is missing. The aircraft's name was only carried on the port side. *GENRIL OOP* was retrofitted with a Cheyenne tail gun position in England. (Karl Hänggi)

2LT Raymond Hoffmann took *SHOO SHOO BABY* to Dübendorf after the number four engine on his B-17G-25-BO (42-31669) lost oil pressure. The Swiss ground crew counted some twelve flak holes in the aricraft. (Karl Hänggi)

In order to save the life of the bombardier, the crew knew their only chance was to head for Switzerland. The bomber was intercepted by Swiss Bf 109Es and escorted to Dübendorf. On final approach, the crew discovered that the ball turret could not be jettisoned and a wheels up landing with the extended turret was not advisable. Instead of landing, the pilots pulled away and circled over the Lake of Zürich. The crew worked to jettison the ball turret. In the meantime, the Officer in Charge at Dübendorf tower gave order for the fighters to shoot the B-17 down because the Swiss believed that the bomber would escape and head back to England.

In fact, the aircraft was in serious trouble and had no intentions of trying to escape. While over the lake, three Bf 109E attacked the helpless bomber. The attack came as a complete surprise to the Americans and they had no opportunity or time to return fire. S/SGT Raymond A. Newall recalled:

The ship was badly damaged and we were preparing for a crash landing when we were attacked by three Swiss fighters without any warning. Their assault set the ship on fire and when we recovered from the attack, the pilot gave the order to bailout.

The fighter attack killed the badly wounded bombardier, Jesse Greenbaum, and the left waist gunner, Richard M. Sendlback. Four of the crew managed to bailout through the main exit hatch but Everett L. Bailey's parachute failed to open and he was killed when he hit a henhouse. The radio operator, William J. Silag, top turret gunner, Raymond A. Newall and right waist gunner, Richard R. Hollingsworth, successfully bailed out and were picked up by Swiss soldiers. The seriously wounded navigator, Charles D. Wallach, was rescued from the bomber which crashed into Lake Greifensee. He was the only survivor of those who went down with the bomber. Four dead bodies were found floating on the lake, but the copilot, James E. Burrey, was still in the aircraft when it was recovered from the bottom of the lake by Martin Schaffner (a Swiss garage owner who became notorious in Switzerland during the early 1950s for recovering bombers from Swiss lakes).

The last aircraft to land was a Fortress of the 92nd Bomb Group named *Butch*. The B-17G-30-BO (42-31914) had been assigned to the

FROSTIE was a B-17G-15-DL (42-37885) Flying Fortress. The aircraft suffered damage to the number one and three engines. 2LT Virgil R. Broyhill landed the ship safely at Dübendorf where the Swiss found some thirty-nine bullet holes. (Karl Hänggi)

"GENRIL OOP" was carried on the port side of the B-17G flown by 2LT Cunningham. All the aircraft's guns have been removed and placed in storage. (Franz Schraner)

326th Bomb Squadron on 11 February 1944. The ship was flown by 2LT Bernard Rosenfeld and his copilot 1LT Gerald H. Robson, Jr. After leaving the target, the formation was attacked by enemy fighters, and *Butch* was seen slowly dropping behind the formation. On approach to Dübendorf, the ship landed too fast and in order to stop the aircraft before it reached the end of the runway, 2LT Rosenfeld retracted the undercarriage, damaging the belly. The bomber was later dismantled and taken to Kloten Air Depot on 16 May 1944.

The growing number of American aircraft in Switzerland (as well as in neutral Sweden) led to investigations by U.S. officials in both countries. Rumors had come through diplomatic channels that in many cases the reasons for a landing were unjustified. Investigations ordered by GEN Spaatz came to the conclusion that few, if any, crews deliberately diverted to Switzerland. Swiss officers were well aware that most aircraft were in fact badly damaged or did not have enough fuel to return to England.

LITTLE CHUB was shot down by Swiss fighters and fell into lake Greifensee while 1LT Everett W. Bailey and his crew were attempting to land at Dübendorf. Martin Schaffner lifted the B-17G-50-BO (42-102446) from the bottom of the lake during the early fifties. The wreckage was later scrapped. (Weltwoche Bilderarchiv)

2LT Bernard Rosenfeld deliberately retracted the undercarriage on his B-17G-30-BO (42-31914) to keep the bomber from overrunning the airfield boundary. The Fortress had a Cheyenne tail gun position and both the chin and ball turret were smashed in the landing. (Fotohaus Wiesner)

25 April 1944

On 25 April 1944, the 8th Air Force sent 199 B-24s of the 2nd Air Division to bomb the rail marshalling yards at Mannheim, while the 1st and 3rd Air Division headed for targets in France. Of the five B-24s reported as missing in action, three diverted to Switzerland. Additionally, a B-24 of the 15th Air Force, which had attacked targets at Turin and Varese, also landed in Switzerland.

The first aircraft to land was *Commando*, a B-24H-1-DT (41-28602) from the 448th Bomb Group, flown by 1LT Henry Schroeder who had flown his B-24 back on three engines the day before. During the flight over France they were fired on by German flak batteries who scored a direct hit on the number two engine which had to be feathered. Later the number three engine began losing power. The Liberator soon became a straggler and to make matters worse, they could not turn back because of strong head winds. The ship was

1LT Henry Schroeder over ran the airfield boundary with his B-24H-1-DT (41-28602) and hit trees. The Liberator had the wing tips ripped off and caught fire. It completely burned and the wreckage was scrapped. (Karl Hanggi)

steadily losing altitude and a decision was made to try to make it to Switzerland. Navigator LT Bruce Crane plotted a course to an airfield east of Lake Neuchatel. Soon after crossing the border they were met by Swiss fighters and escorted to Payerne airfield.

Unfortunately the aircraft was too high on the approach, overran the end of the runway and hit the boundary fence. Schroeder and his copilot, 2LT Lewis M. Sarkovich, managed to control the crash landing, but the wings hit the trees and were ripped from the fuselage. The smashed plane caught fire, but the crew escaped unhurt from the wreckage.

Rum Runner was the other 448th Bomb Group loss that day. This B-24H-1-DT (41-28583) was flown by 1LT Robert E. Lehmann and on this mission the crew was without a bombardier. Lehmann was a highly experienced pilot on four engined bombers since he had flown with Pan American Airways before the war. The aircraft safely landed at Dübendorf with a full bomb load on board. The ten 500 pound bombs were later unloaded with the help of two crew members. No damaged to the Liberator was recorded by the Swiss and there were still some 621 gallons of fuel left in the tanks. The 448th Bomb Group had received a recall signal over France and the rest of the group never went to the target area, since the mission had been cancelled.

The undamaged aircraft was used by the Swiss on several occasions. Two flights were conducted on 8 June 1944. Besides the two Swiss pilots, Oberst Högger and Oberleutnant Heitmaneck, the bomber also carried two American officers acting as instructors.

The 453rd Bomb Group sent twenty-three aircraft out for the Mannheim mission, and two were lost. One of these aircraft was a B-24H-10-CF (42-64496) nicknamed *Borsuk's Bitch*, assigned to 1LT Louis Scherzer who recalled the mission:

1LT Robert E. Lehmann landed *RUM RUNNER* at Dübendorf with a full bomb load aboard. The Swiss found no damage on this B-24H-1-DT (41-28583) and there were still 620 gallons of fuel in the tanks. (Karl Hänggi)

1LT Louis Scherzer's B-24H-10-CF (42-64496) of the 453rd Bomb Group on the runway shortly after its arrival in Switzerland. The aircraft was later repainted with Swiss Air Force markings. (Karl Hänggi)

2LT Leonard S. Houston landed this B-24G-10-NT (42-78184) with the number four engine feathered at the Geneva-Cointrin civil airport.The nose art on *THE ROWDY DOWDYS* was based on a Walt Disney cartoon character. (Peter Schneider)

The aircraft had been experiencing a great deal of electrical problems, which the engineering people were unable to correct. Because of the continuing problem, we had already aborted one mission. On the mission of 25 April, we were on our target bomb run when our Group leader decided to head for a secondary target because of excessive cloud cover over the primary. In heading for the secondary target, we found that we were unable to lower our RPM from the 2,450 rpm to a more normal cruise setting of 1,950 to 2,050 rpm. We tried to start our auxiliary power unit to lower the RPM but we were unsuccessful. It was at that point that the engineer and navigator reported that at our present rate of fuel consumption, it would be impossible to get back to England, so we took up a heading for Switzerland. We were not exactly sure where we were when a Swiss fighter picked us up and directed us to a landing field.

The Liberator came down safely at Dübendorf and saw further use with the Swiss Air Force. On 28 April 1944, the B-24 took off for a flight with Oberst Högger and Wachtmeister Schraner at the controls. The Liberator was later featured in a Swiss propaganda film where the B-24 played the part of an "intruder" which was "forced to land" by Swiss fighters. For the film it carried no group or national markings. The film was made to show Swiss civilians how foreign bombers were forced to land.

The last aircraft down in Switzerland that day came from the 15th Air Force. The ROWDY DOWDYS, a B-24G-10-NT (42-78184) was flown by LT Leonard S. Houston and belonged to the

450th Bomb Group. The Group had been to bomb the Macchi Aircraft Factory near Varese in Northern Italy, close to the Swiss border.

Shortly before reaching the target, the ship was attacked by Messerschmitt Bf 109s. This probably caused some damage, since ten minutes later the number one engine lost power. A few minutes later the number two and four engines also developed problems. With only one engine at full power the ship was steadily losing altitude and the pilot advised the crew to prepare for a bailout. This warning was misunderstood by four of the crew, who abandoned the bomber.

Minutes later two of the engines returned to life but since the aircraft had lost a lot of altitude and had became separated from the formation, the crew decided to head for Switzerland. Additionally, they had been warned that there were still very strong fighter forces in northern Italy making a safe return to their home base nearly impossible.

At 1310 the B-24G-10-NT landed safely at Geneva airfield with the prop feathered on the number four engine. The remaining crew members were: pilot Leonard Houston, copilot 2LT Wesley Urquart, navigator 2LT Morris Lipser and gunners SGTs Albert Lattimer, George Monroe and Benjamin Roderique.

On 14 October 1944, a Swiss Air Force crew ferried the bomber from Geneva to Payerne airfield, where it the remained for the rest of the war. It was returned to Burtonwood, England on 11 October 1945.

1LT Scherzer's B-24H-10-CF (42-64496) had all its American markings overpainted so that the aircraft could be used in a Swiss propaganda film, carrying no national markings. First flight under Swiss control was made on 28 April 1944. (Fotohaus Wiesner)

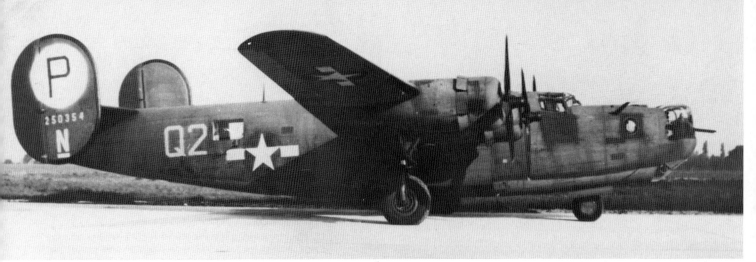

May Landings

Preparations for D-Day kept the 8th Air Force away from Southern Germany and during May only eight American aircraft sought refuge in Switzerland. Two landed on 11 May and six on 27 May, which was the last day American bombers landed in Switzerland before D-Day (6 June 1944).

On 11 May, the 2nd Air Division sent 294 Liberators to a number of important marshalling yards in France. Of the five B-24s reported as missing in action, two made it safely to Switzerland. The first aircraft was a B-24H-10-DT (41-28738) from the 458th Bomb Group. The pilot, Stuart Goldsmith, and his crew named the ship *MEAT AROUND THE CORNER*. The nose art showed a hunter with Adolf Hitler's head in his hand but, in compliance with an order from the Group commander, the Führer's head was replaced by a polecat.

The pilot Stuart Goldsmith recalls:

My crew and I picked up the aircraft when it was brand new and actually took possession of it in San Francisco. We flew it almost exclusively from the time it was manufactured to when it was destroyed on 11 May 1944. We had completed sixteen missions, including the first raid on Berlin and three very memorable raids on Brunswick. On 11 May, we started on an ill-fated mission that would result in the loss of the Liberator. The mission was to Epinal and about twenty minutes before we reached our target, my number three engine oil pressure gauge indicated a dropping pressure. This normally indicated an oil leak requiring the feathering of the propeller. We were able with three engines

2LT William T. Shoup's B-24 H-20-CF (42-50354) *FICKLE FINGER OF FATE* carries the early Group markings and the individual aircraft letter "N" on the fin. The bomber was equipped with armored-back pilot seats, better known as "Coffin Seats" by 8th AF crews. (Karl Hänggi)

to maintain flight and our position in the formation by simply increasing power to the remaining three engines.

After seven or eight minutes, the oil pressure on number two engine began to drop. We had a windmilling propeller which we could no longer feather because all the oil had been lost. We were able to maintain altitude on the remaining two engines; however, the extreme drag of the number two engine meant we would be unable to make it back to our own base in England.

The navigator 2LT William C. Etheredge recalls:

Our engine problems were obviously due to age and overwork. 1LT Stuart Goldsmith asked me how far we could fly over occupied France toward England and as an alternative, to Switzerland. The crew voted to try for the latter rather than become prisoners of the Germans. About the time we crossed into Switzerland, our angle of descent due to the loss of engine power was such that we had to abandon ship. Our plane glided by itself to a crash near a Swiss hospital.

This pretty girl is not what she appears to be. In fact, "she" was 1LT Stuart Goldsmith. He left the Internee Camp at Davos dressed as a peasant woman and then used this disguise to cross the Swiss-French border! (Stuart Goldsmith)

MEAT AROUND THE CORNER is used by 458th BG navigators as a background for a group photo. This B-24H-10-DT (41-28738) crashed at Jegenstorf. The head of Adolf Hitler on the original nose art was later replaced by a Polecat. (Stuart Goldsmith)

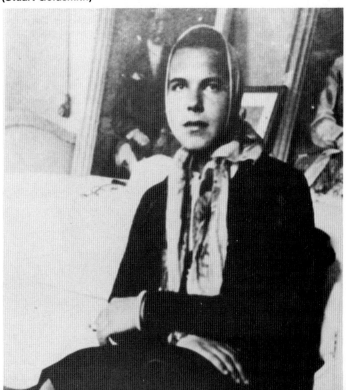

1LT Richard T. Pressey flew *LIBERTY RUN* to Payerne airfield. This B-17G-35-DL (42-107042) diverted to Switzerland after the number one engine lost oil pressure and began running away. (Karl Hänggi)

CAPT Robert D. Brown (second from right) talks with his ground crew in front of his P-51B-5-NA (43-6556) Mustang. He had scored two kills in his Mustang named *CHICAGO GUN MOLL*. CAPT Brown broke a leg when he landed on a tree after bailing out over Switzerland. (Merle Olmsted)

The Liberator crashed into a wooded area near Jegenstorf, while the crew was picked up by Swiss soldiers near Sumiswald.

Stuart Goldsmith told of his stay at Davos:

I became very friendly with a young Swiss Army officer who was in Davos for treatment of tuberculosis of the eye. He would give me French lessons every day and I would teach him English. The officer arranged for me to attend many parties, wearing civilian clothes, at which various Nazi dignitaries were attending. The Germans would come and go, of course not in uniform, living in Switzerland as tourists. It was fascinating talking with and exchanging thoughts with the enemy. My Swiss friend would introduce me as a Swiss from Lausanne and since my French was always better than any of the German's attending the party, they had no reasons to question the authenticity of the claim.

2LT Ralph T. Ritter and I became every more restless and decided we really wanted to get back to our base in England and finish out the twenty-five missions required for a proper discharge. We decided that we could escape past the Swiss guards in Davos dressed as a peasant man and a peasant woman. I tied up my guard in Davos and walked by the very guards and other Swiss people that I had gotten to know during my period of internment, but no one recognized me. Ritter and I made our escape and traveled to Geneva, where we crossed the border. We were met by the French underground in a little town called Mouthe.

The next aircraft to land also took part in the mission to Epinal. The B-24H-20-CF (42-50354) named *Fickle Finger of Fate* was flown by 2LT William T. Shoup and his crew. The crew had come overseas together as part of the original 467th Bomb Group. The navigator, 2LT Robert E. Reno, recalled:

As I recall, the mission went smoothly to target area. After our bombs were dropped, and we were turning back from the

target area, our engineer T/SGT John F. Pollak reported we had sustained damage. It was determined we would not be able to reach the French coast and we headed for Switzerland. We entered Swiss airspace over Fleurier and located Geneva and its airfield. We determined that the landing strip was too short and made a second approach, during which we received some ground fire as we crossed the border at Geneva.

The aircraft was ferried from Geneva airfield to Payerne on 7 October 1944 by Oberst Högger and Wachtmeister Schraner, along with mechanics Spahlinger and Güdel. After the war, it was turned over to American authorities on 11 October 1945.

On 27 May 1944, the 8th Air Force sent 1,126 bomber over the Continent. Most of them were briefed to attack targets in southern Germany and northeastern France. Twenty-four aircraft failed too return; six of them landing in Switzerland.

The first aircraft was a P-51B-5-NA (43-6556) Mustang escort fighter from the 357th Fighter Group. The Group's mission was a fighter escort for the bomber force headed to Ludwigshafen. At 1210, in the vicinity of Strasbourg, France, CAPT Robert D. Brown's *CHICAGO GUN MOLL* was damaged by an enemy fighter. With damage to the rudder control cables and engine, CAPT Brown set course for Switzerland. After crossing the Rhine, he bailed out and parachuted into a tree near the town of Spielhausen breaking his leg. He was given first aid by some local people and he was subsequently taken into the hospital at Wattwil.

CHICAGO GUN MOLL crashed in Winzenberg near Lütisburg, about seventy-five feet from the "Landhaus" Restaurant. Debris from the Mustang caused some damage and set fire to the house, but fortunately none of the guests were hurt.

1LT Richard T. Pressey and his crew were flying a B-17G-35-DL (42-107042) on the way to the chemical works at Ludwigshafen along with the rest of the 91st Bomb Group. The aircraft was named *Liberty*

1LT James Nedrow landed this B-24H-20-FO (42-94946) Liberator named *The Cats* at Payerne with the number four engine feathered. Additionally, the number three engine had also malfunctioned. (Karl Hänggi)

1LT Harold Peters' B-17G-30-BO (42-31899) was heavily damaged by German fighters which knocked out the number three engine. *CHATTERBOX* was on its 19th mission when it was forced to divert to Switzerland. (Karl Hänggi)

This B-17G-20-VE (42-97603) "Mickey" (radar equipped pathfinder) ship was flown by CAPT Norman Radin. It was set on fire by its crew after landing at Knutwil to prevent the secrets of the H2X radar from being discovered by the Swiss. Only the tail remained intact after the fire. (Karl Hänggi)

1LT Robert Daly landed his B-24J-145-CO (44-40102) with the number two engine feathered at Geneva-Cointrin civil airport. The ship carried a mixture of old and new style 2nd Air Division markings. Both waist guns had been thrown out of the aircraft before the landing. (Karl Hänggi)

Run; however, the name was never painted on the Fortress. Richard Pressey recalled the mission:

> *Liberty Run was not the aircraft normally assigned for me to fly. My assigned plane, Roundtrip Topsy, was in the shop to repair flak damage from a previous mission to Cologne. We lost two engines en route to the target and headed for Switzerland. We were intercepted by a Swiss fighter on crossing the border near Base and led to Payerne.*

Another victim on the Ludwigshafen raid was *Chatterbox*, a B-17G-30-BO (42-31899) of the 351st Bomb Group on its nineteenth mission. The bomber was flown by 1LT Harold Peters. Enemy fighters attacked *Chatterbox* and damaged the number three engine, which had to be feathered. The crew set course to Switzerland and landed at Dübendorf at 1229.

During the debriefing held with Swiss officers, the crew was very suspicious and reserved and did not answer questions or fill out the Red Cross forms.

The Cats, a B-24H-20-FO (42-94946), was the only loss for the 458th Bomb Group on the mission to Neunkirchen. Mechanical troubles forced the pilot, 1LT James Nedrow, to feather the propeller on the number four engine. The number three engine began to lose power and for some strange reason the copilot bailed out over France. Republic P-47s escorted the Liberator to Switzerland where Morane fighters of *Fligerkompanie 3* met the B-24 over Berne and guided it to Payerne where a safe landing was made.

Gremlin Buggy II, a B-17G-20-VE (42-97603) was an H2X radar equipped Fortress that was selected to fly as deputy lead for the 94th Bomb Group. Most of the specially trained crew, as well as the aircraft itself, belonged to the 385th Bomb Group. One exception was Command Pilot CAPT William Richards who was from the 94th BG. The Fortress led the wing to the primary target, the marshalling yards at Karlsruhe. The Pathfinder crew, under the command of CAPT Norman I. Radin, had already accomplished nine other missions as a lead crew.

Two navigators were carried, 1LT Robert P. Craig operated the H2X radar and 1LT Garnett Turnstall did the regular navigation. Lead bombardier 1LT James D. Goings recalled the mission:

> *Just as we dropped our bombs, our number two engine was hit. Black smoke poured from it as we dropped out of formation*

and prepared to bailout. After all the oil leaked out, the smoke ceased. The engine windmilled and without lubrication, a terrific vibration soon started. German fighters were in the area, but they did not bother us since we were heading for Switzerland.

The pilot Norman Radin continued:

> *We had no maps of Switzerland, but it was a clear day and we could see Lake Constance. We argued that if we bisected Lake Constance in the center we would be over Switzerland. Our reasoning was correct. We were going to ditch in a lake but at the last moment I decided to land in a farmer's small field with the wheels up. On the final approach, we saw a telephone line which cut the short field in half. Nevertheless, we landed safely in the short space. We set the aircraft on fire because it contained secret H2X radar equipment.*

While the bomber burned at Knutwil, the crew was taken to the "Schweizerhof" hotel at Lucerne for further interrogation by Swiss officials. CAPT Radin later escaped from Switzerland during June of 1944 via Geneva and into occupied France. The rest of the crew was released during the Spring of 1945.

1LT Robert Daly's B-24J-145-CO (44-40102) from the 492nd Bomb Group was the last aircraft to land in Switzerland during May. Just as the Group hit the IP, Daly lost the number three engine. A short time later the number two engine had to be shut down. A hurried check revealed that the cause was complete fuel starvation. Before the engineer could complete a fuel transfer hookup, the other inboard engine quit for the same reason and the lagging Liberator was discovered by a number of Luftwaffe fighters. Some quick computations on the range of their aircraft with the fuel remaining on board offered only two alternatives — part way to England or all the way to Switzerland. Daly set the ship down at Geneva-Cointrin air field. There was no damage to the Liberator and on 7 October 1944, Oberst Högger flew the Liberator from Geneva to Payerne where the bomber remained for the rest of the war.

June Arrivals

D-Day and the following weeks kept the 8th Air Force away from Southern Germany and only one aircraft sought refuge in Switzerland during June. This aircraft was joined by three 15th Air Force aircraft that all arrived on the same day.

On 13 June, B-17s and B-24s attacked the Bavarian capital of Munich. The first Liberator to land in Switzerland was 2LT Edward Eibs's B-24H-15-FO (42-52661). On the Munich mission, the supercharger on the number one engine went out over Caorle, Italy. Over the target the bomb bay doors failed to open and the bomb load was dropped through the closed doors. As the formation turned for home, Messerschmitt Bf 109s and Me 410s attacked the 484th Bomb Group. For some reason, two of the crew (the navigator, 2LT Prodgers and one of the gunners, SGT Storer) left the ship over Germany. A shortage of fuel and a malfunctioning engine forced the crew to land at Dübendorf airfield at 1028.

BELLE RINGER, a B-24H-15-FO (42-52347) of the 460th BG, was another victim of the Munich raid. This battered Liberator was flown by 1LT Erwin Janoviak. A loss of oil pressure on the number one engine forced the pilot to feather the propeller. This, in addition to a shortage of fuel, led the crew to land in Switzerland instead of crossing the Alps. The Liberator touched down at Dübendorf at 1051.

The sole B-17 Flying Fortress to arrive in June landed under somewhat strange circumstances. *Ole Ironsides*, a B-17G-30-BO (42-31865) from the 463rd Bomb Group, was flown by 2LT Lester F. Weaver. After crossing the Alps from the target, the crew noticed a failure in the oxygen system, as well as in the radios. Rather than flying alone to Celone, the crew decided to land in Switzerland. For a while, the bomber circled with the landing gear down over the Swiss-Italian border, looking for a suitable place to land. A Morane fighter guided the B-17G to Magadino where a normal landing was accomplished.

The crew was interrogated by Swiss officials and was later visited by the U.S. Vice-consul James Christy Bell. The bomber was parked in front of the two wooden hangars at Magadino and kept under guard until 16 June 1944, when a Swiss ferry crew under the command of Oberst Högger flew the B-17 from Magadino to Dübendorf. These

2LT Edward Eibs had to drop the bombs thru the closed bomb bay doors when the doors jammed over the target. A fuel shortage forced the B-24H-15-FO (42-52661) Liberator to land at Dübendorf. (Karl Hänggi)

1LT Erwin Janoviak landed his B-24H-15-FO (42-52347) at Dübendorf with number one propeller feathered. On 27 September 1945 the Liberator named *BELLE RINGER* taxied out for a ferry flight to Burtonwood, England. The B-24 ran out of fuel in bad weather and was completely destroyed on a crash landing near Paris. (Fotohaus Wiesner)

ferry flights required some precautions. It was necessary to inform all the anti-aircraft units about the route, the time and date the bomber was to be ferried from one place to another. Shortly after takeoff the bomber received some friendly anti-aircraft fire near Biasca, even though Swiss markings were painted on the Fortress. Luckily for the Swiss crew, no one was injured and the aircraft received only minor damage. The Fortress made a safe landing at Dübendorf at 1624.

On 28 June 1944, 378 Liberators of the 2nd Air Division took off to bomb the marshalling yard at Saarbrücken, Germany. The only loss for the entire force was lucky enough to land in Switzerland. 1LT Lloyd A. Saari's B-24H-25-FO (42-95056) was on its 24th mission. The crew had flown a number of missions in a short time, including two on D-Day. On the Saarbrücken mission the Liberator did not carry a ball turret. During a German attack the Liberator was hit in the number two engine, which lost oil pressure, causing the propeller to be feathered. Then the supercharger on the number three engine began to malfunction. 1LT Saari headed for Switzerland and destroyed all important documents and blew up the secret Gee-Device. At 0840 the Liberator touched ground at Payerne airfield in western Switzerland. The Swiss interrogation officers found the crew to be in a rather exhausted condition.

2LT Lester Weaver landed this B-17G-30-BO (42-31865) at Magadino due a failure of the oxygen system. *Ole Ironsides* was shot at by friendly anti-aircraft units when its Swiss crew ferried the ship from Magadino to Dübendorf on 16 June 1944. (Karl Hänggi)

1LT Lloyd A. Saari landed his B-24H-25-FO (42-95056) Liberator at Payerne with the number two engine feathered. Additionally, the Liberator had problems with the supercharger on the number three engine. (Karl Hänggi)

11 July 1944

On 11 July 1944, the 8th Air Force started a series of three attacks against Munich and other targets in southern Germany. These missions brought another large number of American aircraft to Switzerland. On 11 July, 1,176 B-17s and B-24s were dispatched to the marshalling yards at Munich, the Bavarian Motors Works (BMW) at Munich Allach and the Munich-Riem airfield. Munich, as the birth place of the National Socialist Party had a special significance for the Nazis, who called the Bavarian capital *Stadt der Bewegung* (City of the Movement). The destruction of Munich by allied forces was both strategic and political.

Of 1,176 bombers that left England that morning, twenty failed to return, but eight made it to Switzerland.

The first aircraft which sought refuge was *PICCADILLY ANN II*, a B-17G-55-BO (42-102651) of the 447th Bomb Group. The ship had already flown ten previous missions and on this one was flown by 1LT Herbert Altman, who recalled the mission:

> *PICCADILLY ANN II was not the ship we regularly flew. When it was flyable we flew Bouncing Baby. The decision to come to Switzerland was made by myself, copilot Leebert W. McFarland and our navigator, Theodore Hocking. On final approach to Dübendorf airfield, the local airfield flak began to fire at us but no hits were scored.*

The Swiss ground crew noted no damage on the aircraft, but the propeller on the number three engine had been feathered due to a loss of oil in that engine.

1LT Herbert Altman's B-17G-55-BO (42-102651) on the grass shortly after it landed at Dübendorf. *PICCADILLY ANN II* diverted to Switzerland after the number three engine failed. (Karl Hänggi)

The nosewheel collapsed on 2LT John C. Tracey's B-24J-150-CO (44-40168) when he landed at Dübendorf with the number two engine feathered and the number four engine losing oil. *Tequila Daisy* was named after a drink the original crew had in a bar at Juarez, Mexico while training in Texas. (Karl Hänggi)

This B-17G-55-BO (42-102651) in storage at Dübendorf with all its guns removed was named *PICCADILLY ANN II*. The Fortress was on its 10th mission when it diverted to Switzerland. (Franz Schraner)

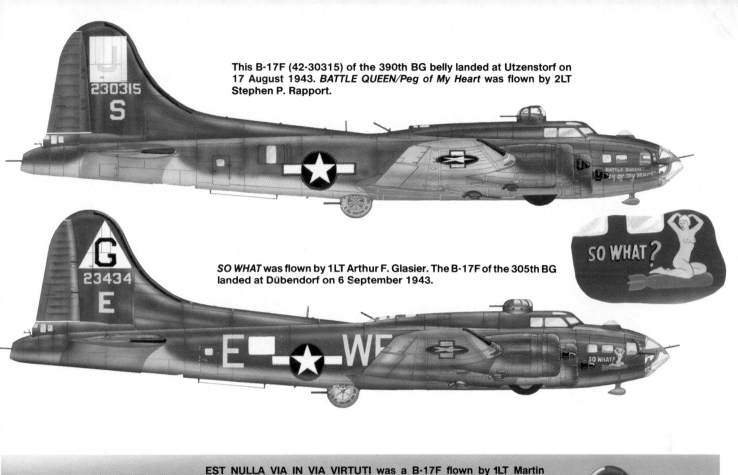

This B-17F (42-30315) of the 390th BG belly landed at Utzenstorf on 17 August 1943. *BATTLE QUEEN/Peg of My Heart* was flown by 2LT Stephen P. Rapport.

SO WHAT was flown by 1LT Arthur F. Glasier. The B-17F of the 305th BG landed at Dübendorf on 6 September 1943.

EST NULLA VIA IN VIA VIRTUTI was a B-17F flown by 1LT Martin Andrews. The aircraft landed at Magadino on 6 September 1943. The aircraft was repainted in Swiss markings for the ferry flight to Emmen on 22 October 1943.

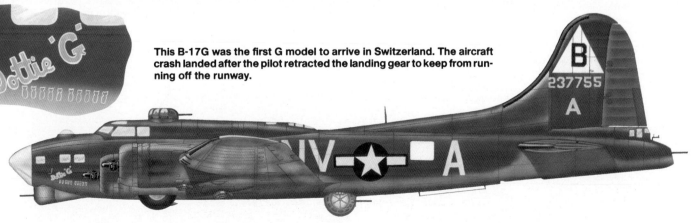

This B-17G was the first G model to arrive in Switzerland. The aircraft crash landed after the pilot retracted the landing gear to keep from running off the runway.

The nosewheel on 1LT Robert a. Gallups B-24H-2-FO (42-7571) failed when he overshot the runway at Dübendorf and ended in the corn field. *LILLIAN ANN II* had the number three engine feathered. (Karl Hänggi)

Manchester Leader, a B-17G-20-DL (42-37976) would also end this day in Switzerland. This combat veteran had been assigned to the 92nd Bomb Group on 8 January 1944 and had already flown forty-five missions. The pilot, 2LT John R. Seilheimer recalled the mission:

> *Over the target, we lost two of our engines and we fired the colored flares for the day informing the formation that we needed fighter escort and were heading for Switzerland. We were escorted by five P-51s to the Swiss border. We were preparing to make a two engine landing when Swiss fighters appeared and fired at us. We could see the tracers passing us. As they passed, the anti-aircraft gun barrage began. The first series took off the last three feet of the left wing. That was a jolting shock! The next series left a two foot hole just behind the copilot. The next series took out the radio room. As we turned onto final, the fighters reappeared firing tracers all the way down. A landing was managed. The Swiss guards boarded the ship through the radio room with tommy guns and fire extinguishers and extinguished the oxygen fed fire.*

Tequila Daisy was a B-24J-150-CO (44-40168) of the ill-fated 492nd Bomb Group. The Liberator was flown by 2LT John C. Tracey and carried no bombardier on this mission. Accurate flak over the target knocked out the number two and four engines, leaving Switzerland as the only alternative for the crew. As the bomber touched down, the nosewheel collapsed, damaging the nose section. Mechanics cut out the name and the piece of skin is now on display at the Swiss Air Force Museum at Dübendorf.

The 392nd Bomb Group lost two ships in the raid, but both made it to Altenrhein airfield. 1LT Siegvard J. Robertson's B-24H-25-DT (42-51106) was hit by flak in the number four engine over the target area. He dropped out of formation and radioed his intentions of going to Switzerland. After crossing the border, Swiss AA units fired at the Liberator. The pilot circled for some fifteen minutes over Altenrhein before he decided to land. During the landing the nosewheel collapsed. The B-24H was later repaired by Swiss mechanics and on 30 August 1944, Oberst Högger and Wachtmeister Schraner ferried the bomber from Altenrhein to Dübendorf.

1LT George L. Bridson's B-24H-25-FO (42-95033) of the 392nd BG was a squadron lead ship and carried two navigators, 1LT Ralph L. White and 1LT Santo Italia. Flak damaged the number one engine which had to be feathered and the number two engine which

was windmilling, producing a lot of drag. As on 1LT Robertson's aircraft, the nosewheel also collapsed on Bridson's Liberator. The B-24H was repaired and finally ferried to Dübendorf on 7 September 1944.

1LT Robert A. Gallup's B-24H-2-FO (42-7571) had some trouble with the number one and three engines before the 445th BG formation reached the target. *Lillian Ann II* also flew without a navigator. The engine troubles got worse when the supercharger on the number one engine failed and, after bombs away, the number three engine had to be feathered because of flak damage. With only two engines left, the crew decided to fly to Switzerland. They circled for about thirty minutes over Switzerland before Swiss fighters appeared and guided them down to Dübendorf. Unfortunately, the Liberator landed long and ran into a corn field, where the nosewheel collapsed.

1LT Saul Platinsky's B-24H-25-FO (42-95196) was the other 492nd BG aircraft that landed in Switzerland that day. On the way to the target, the pilots lost control over the number two engine which ran away and could not be stopped. As a result, the pilot lost the formation and decided to fly to Switzerland.

After crossing the border, the Liberator was shot at by Swiss anti-aircraft guns in the area of Weinfelden. 1LT Platinsky immediately lowered the undercarriage as a sign of surrender, but the flak did not stop. He began to fire flares every five seconds, but even this did not help. Finally, they past out of range. Platinsky was about to give the bailout order when Swiss fighters appeared and escorted the bomber to Dübendorf.

The last landing of the day was by B-17G-15-DL (42-37873) of the 447th BG, flown by 2LT Robert M. Jacobs. The Fortress had experienced a lot of trouble with its engines all the way to the target. Shortly after

MANCHESTER LEADER landed with its number three engine feathered. Additionally, the number one engine had lost a lot of oil. Swiss anti-aircraft gun fire caused the damage to the fuselage of this B-17G-20-DL (42-37976) flown by 2LT John R. Seilheimer. (Fotohaus Wiesner)

1LT Saul Platinsky landed his overall Natural Metal B-24H-25-FO (42-95196) Liberator at Dübendorf due to engine trouble and flak damage. No other damage was found by the Swiss ground crew. (Karl Hänggi)

The nosewheel on this B-24H-25-DT (42-51106) collapsed during its landing at Altenrhein. The last three digits on the serial number were repeated on the nose in Black. The pilot, 1LT Siegvart J. Robertson, diverted with the Liberator when the number four engine developed a serious oil leak. (Karl Hänggi)

leaving the target, the ship left the formation and proceeded in the general direction of Switzerland. Four P-51s escorted the B-17 to the border and, without a Swiss fighter escort, the crew found Dübendorf, making a safe landing at 1352. Swiss ground crews recorded no damage to the aircraft.

This B-17G-15-DL (42-37873) was flown by 2LT Robert Jacobs. A lack of fuel forced him to land at Dübendorf where no other damage was recorded by the Swiss. The aircraft has an unusual starboard cheek gun arrangement, typical of early B-17Gs. The front window has been enlarged and angled outward to accommodate the gun. On later Gs it was the center window on the starboard side that was enlarged for a gun. (Karl Hänggi)

PICCADILLY ANN II was an overall Natural Metal B-17G of the 710th BS, 447th BG, 8th AF. The aircraft landed at Dübendorf on 11 July 1944.

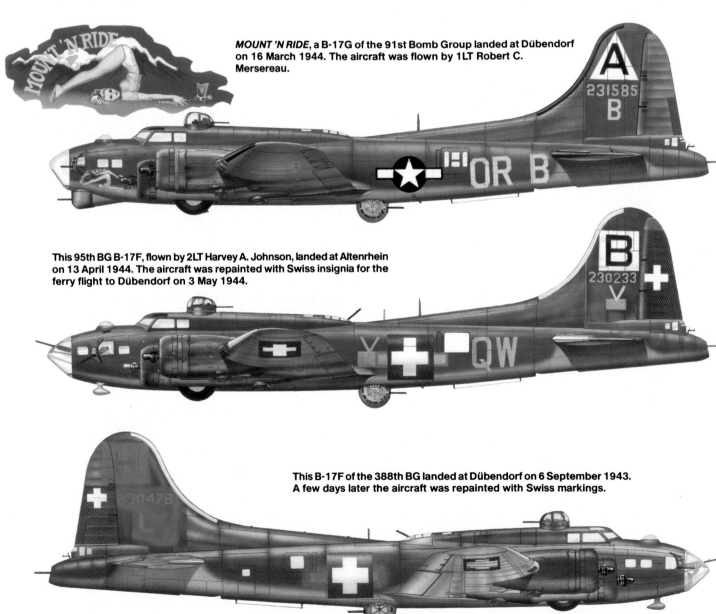

MOUNT 'N RIDE, a B-17G of the 91st Bomb Group landed at Dübendorf on 16 March 1944. The aircraft was flown by 1LT Robert C. Mersereau.

This 95th BG B-17F, flown by 2LT Harvey A. Johnson, landed at Altenrhein on 13 April 1944. The aircraft was repainted with Swiss insignia for the ferry flight to Dübendorf on 3 May 1944.

This B-17F of the 388th BG landed at Dübendorf on 6 September 1943. A few days later the aircraft was repainted with Swiss markings.

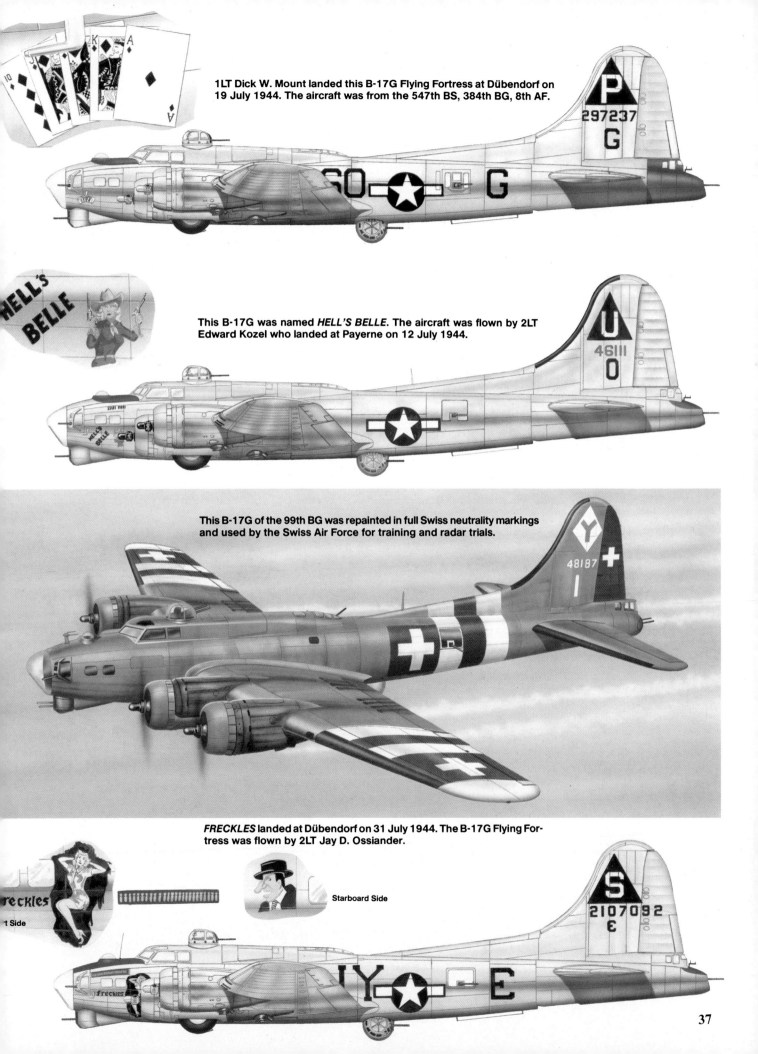

1LT Dick W. Mount landed this B-17G Flying Fortress at Dübendorf on 19 July 1944. The aircraft was from the 547th BS, 384th BG, 8th AF.

This B-17G was named *HELL'S BELLE*. The aircraft was flown by 2LT Edward Kozel who landed at Payerne on 12 July 1944.

This B-17G of the 99th BG was repainted in full Swiss neutrality markings and used by the Swiss Air Force for training and radar trials.

FRECKLES landed at Dübendorf on 31 July 1944. The B-17G Flying Fortress was flown by 2LT Jay D. Ossiander.

Starboard Side

t Side

Wachtmeister Schraner, the Liberator's copilot (right) just after landing at Dübendorf with B-24H-25-FO (42-95033). He ferried the ship along with the pilot, Oberst Högger, from Altenrhein to Dübendorf on 7 September 1944. (Franz Schraner)

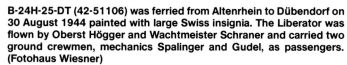

B-24H-25-DT (42-51106) was ferried from Altenrhein to Dübendorf on 30 August 1944 painted with large Swiss insignia. The Liberator was flown by Oberst Högger and Wachtmeister Schraner and carried two ground crewmen, mechanics Spalinger and Gudel, as passengers. (Fotohaus Wiesner)

1LT George L. Bridson flew this B-24H-25-FO (42-95033) to Altenrhein, where the nosewheel collapsed. After replacing the badly leaking number one engine with one taken from an Olive Drab Liberator, the ship was ferried to Dübendorf. (Fotohaus Wiesner)

12 July 1944

On this day, the 8th Air Force sent 1,402 bombers against Munich and twenty-four of them failed to return. Of these, ten made it to Switzerland. The first aircraft was *Gloria*, a B-17G-50-BO (42-102457) flown by 2LT Wendell O. Scott. *GLORIA* had been originally assigned to Frank A. Bartos who had named the ship after his wife. Over Mannheim, LT Scott called the Group leader and stated he was losing an engine and could not keep up with the formation. He then headed for Switzerland with a fighter escort where a safe landing was made at Dübendorf. The Swiss noted that number two and three engines were inoperative and there were four flak holes in the aircraft.

1LT Gordon W. MacDonald's B-24H-25-DT (42-51113) was the only loss for the 491st BG that day. The ground crew had been working on the engines of this aircraft until just prior to departure. MacDonald and his crew were flying the Liberator for the first time and were carrying no bombardier. Near Stuttgart, the aircraft began having trouble with the oil pressure on both the number one and number two engines. Finally, the propeller on number one had to be feathered. As a result, they lost altitude and were unable to keep up with the formation. They salvoed their bombs and made a 180 degree turn for Switzerland, where a safe landing was made at Payerne.

2LT Gerald L. Kerr and his crew were flying their B-17G-20-BO (42-31552) Flying Fortress for only the second time, all their previous missions having been flown in an older Flying Fortress. The tail gunner, S/SGT Donald B. Boyle, recalled the fateful mission:

Just as we started our bomb run over Munich, we were hit by anti-aircraft fire which knocked out two engines. No one was injured and our pilot ordered the bombs to be jettisoned. We picked up two of our fighters for escort and headed for Switzerland. We made it to the mountains, losing altitude all the way and the fighters gave us a heading and left us. When we got into the

FAT STUFF II was a B-24H-2-FO (42-7591) Liberator. On 12 July 1944 this combat veteran sought refuge in Switzerland. Part of the nose art had been covered by add-on armor plating designed to protect the cockpit area. (USAF)

2LT George W. Wilson and his crew line up *FAT STUFF II* **on final approach to Altenrhein airfield at 1404, 12 July 1944. The aircraft had a damaged number two engine. (Mattias Weichelt)**

mountains, we were lower than some of the mountain peaks and we were flying in and out of snow squalls. The plane was sagging to the left as the two port side engines were the ones that were out. It was only through the great skill of our pilot, LT Kerr, that we had made it this far.

At around 1400, because of the snow making visibility poor and our third engine starting to throw oil, we were ordered to bailout. The waist gunner, S/SGT Harold E. Ahlfors, ball turret gunner, S/SGT Samuel P. Younger; radio operator, T/SGT Ernest J. Hegedus; and myself parachuted out. We all landed in German occupied territory and were taken prisoner within the hour and spent the rest of the war as POWs.

2LT Wendell Scott landed at Dübendorf with the number two and three engines feathered on his B-17G-50-BO (42-102457). Later, both engines on *GLORIA* **were repaired by Swiss ground crews. (Fotohaus Wiesner)**

2LT Edward Kozel landed his Natural Metal B-17G-40-DL (44-6111) Fortress named *HELL'S BELLE* **at Payerne after anti-aircraft fire blew off the propeller from the number one engine. (Herr Muller)**

39

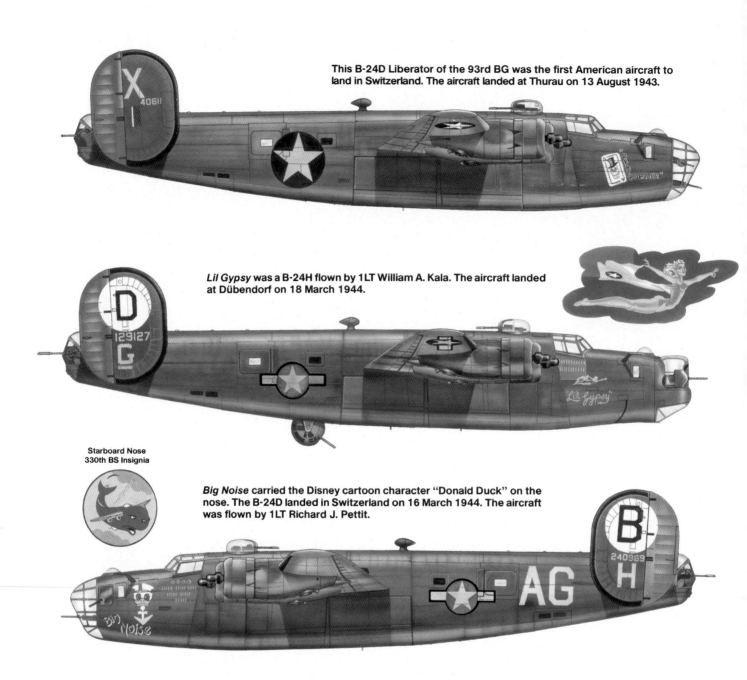

This B-24D Liberator of the 93rd BG was the first American aircraft to land in Switzerland. The aircraft landed at Thurau on 13 August 1943.

Lil Gypsy was a B-24H flown by 1LT William A. Kala. The aircraft landed at Dübendorf on 18 March 1944.

Starboard Nose
330th BS Insignia

Big Noise carried the Disney cartoon character "Donald Duck" on the nose. The B-24D landed in Switzerland on 16 March 1944. The aircraft was flown by 1LT Richard J. Pettit.

This B-24H landed at Altenrhein on 11 July 1944 and suffered a collapsed nosewheel. The aircraft was flown by 1LT Siegvard J. Robertson. After repairs, the aircraft was repainted in Swiss markings and ferried to Dübendorf.

Belle Ringer was a B-24H of the 763rd BS, 460th BG. She landed at Dübendorf on 13 June 1944.

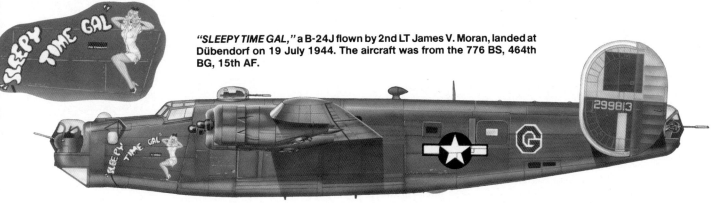

"SLEEPY TIME GAL," a B-24J flown by 2nd LT James V. Moran, landed at Dübendorf on 19 July 1944. The aircraft was from the 776 BS, 464th BG, 15th AF.

This B-24H was named *"BOMBS AWAY"* and was flown by 1st LT Herbert Hopkins. The aircraft landed at Payerne on 12 July 1944.

2LT Harry Schultz landed this B-24G Liberator of the 825th BS, 484th BG, 15th AF at Dübendorf on 3 August 1944.

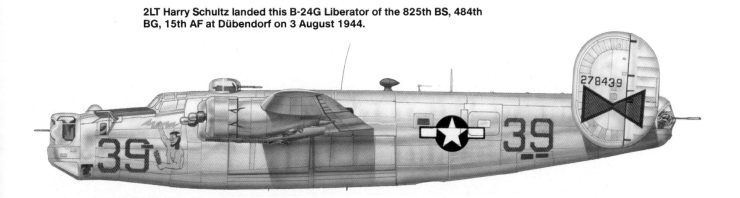

2LT Gerald L. Kerr and two other officers were killed when this B-17G-20-BO (42-31552) Flying Fortress crashed into a mountainside on 12 July 1944. The only part of the aircraft that was still recognizable was the tail section. (Fotohaus Wiesner)

Later I learned from our top turret man, T/SGT Leon Finnerman, that after we jumped, the weather cleared enough so that the pilot thought they could make it. But within minutes, the third engine cut out and they prepared to jump. Finneran jumped and the copilot 2LT Arthur H. Lindskoog jumped behind him. Finneran made it safely to the ground and was found some hours later by the Swiss military. Within seconds, the plane crashed with the pilot, LT Kerr; the bombardier, 2LT Melvin L. Levine; and the navigator, 2LT Edward A. Schilling still aboard. Finneran said he heard the crash and saw the smoke as he floated down.

Unfortunately, the copilot's parachute failed to open and his body was found on 20 July about 2,100 feet away from the mountainside where the B-17 crashed. The bodies of the four dead crew members were taken by Swiss soldiers to Klosters and eventually buried at Münsingen.

FAT STUFF II, a B-24H-2-FO (42-7591) of the 448th Bomb Group, was flown by 2LT George Wilson. The right waist gunner, SGT Rocky Starek, recalled their mission:

On that last mission, after our plane was crippled by antiaircraft fire on the outskirts of Munich, we dropped out of formation. A P-51 Mustang joined us and flew with us for a short while. He asked our pilot if we could make it to Italy, and the answer was no. LT Wilson then asked the navigator 2LT R.J. Ginn to lay out a course to Switzerland, since it was already determined we could only make it as far as Belgium. As we turned for Switzerland, the P-51 wished us luck and departed.

A Swiss Corporal relaxes on the tail of a B-17G-40-VE (42-97957). The aircraft, flown by 2LT John O'Hara, landed at Payerne on 12 July with two engines out. The Flying Fortress in the background was *HELL'S BELLE* of the 457th BG. (Herr Muller)

LT Kerr's B-17G-20-BO (42-31552) on the ramp at its home base of Glatton, England shortly after the 457th Bomb Group arrived in England during January 1944. Six months later the Fortress would be lost over Switzerland.

As we neared the Swiss border, we saw a group of German soldiers with a Red Cross laid out and they were firing red flares as though to entice us to land. Luckily for us, our pilot decided to fly on and we landed in a swampy field near Altenrhein. We were told later it was one of the shortest landings ever made by a B-24.

2LT John P. O'Hare's B-17G-40-VE (42-97957) Fortress had trouble with the pitch control mechanism of propellers one and four on the way to the target. Enemy attacks caused further damage to the number one engine and to the airframe. As a result, the pilot left the formation for Switzerland and made a safe landing at Payerne with the number one prop feathered and the number four propeller damaged from the inoperative pitch control.

Miss Fortune, a B-24H-15-FO (42-52559) of the 467th BG, was another ship which did not make it back to England that day. The pilot, 1LT Richard E. Evans and his crew ran into trouble when the number two engine lost a lot of oil and the number four propeller had to be feathered due to mechanical problems. On the way to Switzerland, the crew threw all the ammunition and the two waist guns out of the aircraft. The Liberator made a safe landing at Dübendorf.

The nose art on *BOMBS AWAY* was painted by SGT J.P. Johansen. 1LT Herbert Hopkins landed the B-24H-25-FO (42-95096) Liberator at Payerne airfield with two engines knock out. (Herr Muller)

1LT Gordon W. MacDonald had no oil pressure on either the number one or number two engines on his B-24H-25-DT (42-51113) but made a safe landing at Payerne on 12 July. (Karl Hänggi)

Miss Fortune was flown by 1LT Richard E. Evans. The aircraft landed with the number four engine feathered and the number two engine leaking oil. The rear bomb bay door is natural metal on this otherwise camouflaged B-24H-15-FO (42-52559). (Karl Hänggi)

Another ship in trouble was 1LT Thomas P. Vann's B-24H-20-DT (41-28948). The copilot 2LT Robert N. Stone told of the mission:

Before we reached the bomb release point, we encountered heavy anti-aircraft fire and one burst struck our number three engine causing us to shut it down. Increased power setting on the remaining engines enabled us to remain in the formation and to proceed on to the target. Just a few moments before "bombs away," we were struck by flak again damaging the supercharger on our number four engine and the fuselage in the area of the navigator's position and copilot's seat. Our navigator, 1LT Leon Rosenthal was wounded in the face and hands by shrapnel and plexiglas bits from a nearby window. I was struck in the foot and leg with shrapnel. We were able to drop our bombs as planned and then, on turning off the target, we found we were not going to be able to remain at the altitude with the loss of power and of course we would not enjoy the protection of the formation for the return home.

We did not have much of an alternative. The odds were that we would be shot down after we lagged behind the formation and lost altitude. We would be very vulnerable to fighter attack if we tried to get over the Channel and perhaps have to ditch in the water. A quick vote was taken among the crew and the vote was nine to one that we turn for Switzerland and land at Dübendorf. We signaled for a fighter escort to the Swiss border, using a Green/Green Very pistol flare. We picked up a couple of P-51 fighters and got over to the Swiss border.

We found the weather conditions had deteriorated there and proceeded to Basel, where we easily found the airport. But, here again, we met the Germans. We erred in flying over their side of the Rhine while we were preparing to land, and they promptly saluted us with many rounds of fairly accurate anti-aircraft fire.

We noted that the Germans were trying to lure us to their side of the Rhine by waving to us and proudly displaying the flags of the International Red Cross, which is the reverse of the Swiss national Flag. We sorted that out in a hurry and proceeded to land in Basel.

BIM BAM BOLA, a B-24H-15-FO (42-94735) of the 448th bomb Group was hit by anti-aircraft fire over Munich, which knocked out the number three engine. 1LT Billie C. Blanton immediately left the formation and headed for Switzerland. Over the Lake Constance area the entire crew left the Liberator which crashed at Fideris-Küblis at 1530.

Unfortunately, only half of the crew landed in Switzerland. Billie C. Blanton, copilot 2LT Edwin F. Hewitt, engineer S/SGT Adrian J. Denbroeder and left waist gunner SGT Armor L. McKain were fortunate. While navigator 2LT George E. Klein, radio operator S/SGT Robert P. Larson, nose turret gunner SGT Paul E. Sherlock, tail gunner SGT Salvatore J. Sparacio and left waist gunner SGT Bernard Stelzer were captured by the Germans.

2LT Edward Kozel's B-17G-40-DL (44-6111) was hit while on the bomb run and a piece of flak literally cut away the propeller on the number one engine. Kozel dropped *HELL'S BELLE* out of formation and headed for Switzerland. Kozel made a landing at Payerne airfield. Later the Swiss replaced the defective engine and ferried the bomber to Dübendorf.

1LT Herbert Hopkins had a lot of trouble with the number two and three engines on the way to the target. He was flying *BOMBS AWAY*, a B-24H-25-FO (42-95096) of the 458th BG based at Horsham. The number two engine steadily lost oil and the number three engine had no oil pressure. With two damaged engines and an insufficient fuel supply to make it back home, the crew decided to fly to Switzerland. Over Lake Neuchatel, they were picked up by Moranes of *Fliegerkompanie* 18 and guided to Payerne, where they made a safe landing.

1LT Thomas Vann's B-24H-20-DT (41-28948) was warming up for the ferry flight from Basel-Birsfelden airfield to Dübendorf. To lighten the ship, the upper turret, guns, radios and armor were removed. (Fotohaus Wiesner)

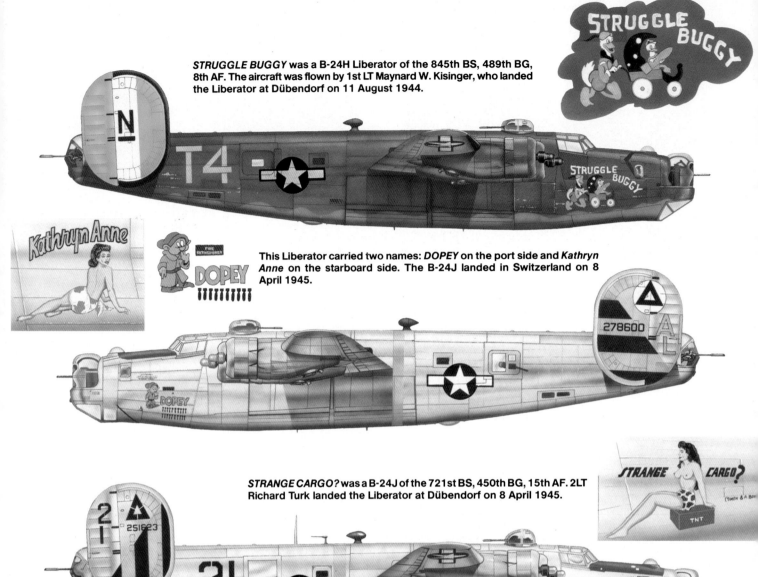

STRUGGLE BUGGY was a B-24H Liberator of the 845th BS, 489th BG, 8th AF. The aircraft was flown by 1st LT Maynard W. Kisinger, who landed the Liberator at Dübendorf on 11 August 1944.

This Liberator carried two names: *DOPEY* on the port side and *Kathryn Anne* on the starboard side. The B-24J landed in Switzerland on 8 April 1945.

STRANGE CARGO? was a B-24J of the 721st BS, 450th BG, 15th AF. 2LT Richard Turk landed the Liberator at Dübendorf on 8 April 1945.

Although the Swiss repainted this Liberator with full neutrality markings for its ferry flight to Dübendorf, the aircraft was still fired on by Swiss anti-aircraft gunners.

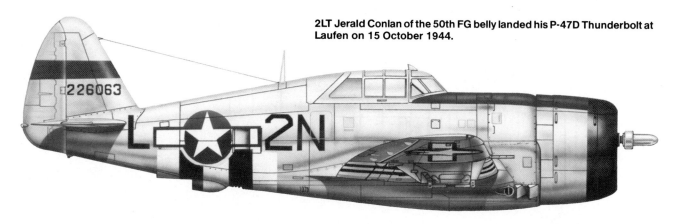

2LT Jerald Conlan of the 50th FG belly landed his P-47D Thunderbolt at Laufen on 15 October 1944.

CAPT Robert Brown bailed out of his P-51B named *CHICAGO GUN MOLL* over Switzerland on 27 May 1944. He broke his leg on landing.

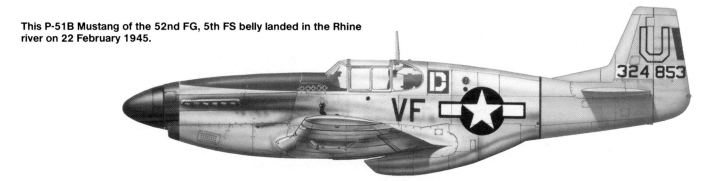

This P-51B Mustang of the 52nd FG, 5th FS belly landed in the Rhine river on 22 February 1945.

The Swiss Air Force repaired and test flew this P-51B. The aircraft, flown by 1LT Curtis Simpson, had made a forced landing at Ems/Plaraga on 19 July 1944.

13 July 1944

On 13 July, the 1st and 3rd Air Divisions once again attacked Munich, while the 2nd Air Division was sent to the marshalling yards at Saarbrücken. In all some 1,043 bombers participated in the raid; ten were lost, but five of these managed to reach Switzerland.

2LT Dale E. Grubb's B-24H-20-FO (42-94989) became a victim of the anti-aircraft fire over Saarbrücken and the number four engine was on fire as he left the formation southeast of the target. Shortly after crossing the Swiss border, Grubb gave order to bailout. About 600 feet from the town of Bätterkinden, the ship exploded raining the town with countless small pieces of aircraft. One of the crew members was slightly injured and taken to the hospital at Solothurn, while the rest of the crew was taken to Emmen for further interrogation.

1LT Robert G. Turner's B-17G-35-DL (42-107031) encountered heavy anti-aircraft fired over the target, which knocked out the number four engine. At 0952 he left the formation near Munich and headed for Switzerland with a P-51 Mustang escort. Turner circled over Switzerland for some thirty minutes before Swiss fighters picked him up and guided him to Dübendorf, where a safe landing was made on three engines.

Another victim of the flak over the target was 1LT Paul H. Long's B-17G-35-VE (42-97905). He flew in the No 4 position in the 41st Combat Wing, which was led by a B-17 from 305th BG, although the rest of the formation was supplied by the 303rd Bomb Group. At 0942 hours, the aircraft was hit by flak which tore a big hole in the wing between the number one and the number two engines. After

Flak ruptured the right wing tanks on this B-17G-35-DL (42-107137). 1LT Charles Harding and his crew jettisoned the ball turret before landing at Payerne. This 100th BG Flying Fortress was the last B-17 to leave Switzerland for Burtonwood after the war, departing on 11 October 1945. (Karl Hänggi)

leaving the target area, Long left the formation and was seen by other ships headed toward Switzerland with fuel leaking from the wing. The landing at Dübendorf was far from easy. The number two engine had to be shut down and the number one engine was damaged. Additionally, the flaps were inoperative, which necessitated that the final approach was made at very high speed. The ship overran the runway and finally came to a halt in a meadow. An examination by Swiss engineers revealed that the port wing had been hit by two shells and there were some sixty shrapnel holes in the wing.

The last landings of the day were made by two 100th Bomb Group aircraft. 2LT Donald A. Waters was flying a B-17G-1-BO (42-31074) named *CAHEPIT* (an abbreviation of "Cannot help it"). The pilot Donald Waters recalled:

I flew five missions in the Fortress and many practice flights. It was one of the oldest airplanes in the group and was considered a "practice" airplane. It flew like a truck at low altitude, but at high altitude up to 25,000 feet it (for me) flew much better than the newer G-models. So I wanted to fly it in combat. We had bombed Munich and the airplane was pretty badly shot up by flak. With only one and a half engines left and other troubles, it was totally impossible to reach England.

Switzerland was the best alternative and it was real close. Shortly after crossing Lake Constance at 13,000 feet, the clouds

1LT Paul Long's B-17G-35-VE (42-97905) Fortress suffered heavy flak damage over the target, causing the number two engine to be feathered. The Fortress overran the runway at Dübendorf due to flak damage to its flaps. (Karl Hänggi)

Flak damage on LT Long's B-17G-35-VE (42-97905). Shrapnel from two shell bursts cut a large hole in the wing between the number one and number two engines. The crew reported seeing daylight thru the wing. (Fotohaus Wiesner)

Before dawn on 22 May, an intruding Luftwaffe Junkers Ju 88 dropped several small bombs on the 385th BG's base at Great Ashfield. One of the bombs exploded near a B-17G-35-DL (42-107031) that would land in Switzerland a few weeks after this incident. (USAF)

thickened into an undercast. Four Me-109s of the Swiss Air Force started to "Jump" me so I dove thru the clouds and lost the 109s but found myself trapped by the mountains. I could no longer fly over them with the little power left from the engines. Smoke, and later fire were coming from both wingtips. I had to land really quick! Up ahead my copilot spotted a landing strip. I took a quick look at it and headed for it. As it was on my right (I was in the left seat) I could not get a good look at the strip until I had turned on final approach. When I finally got "my head out" I saw to my surprise that I was coming in to a very short (1,200 feet) strip that was across the valley. A nice longer strip that ran up and down the valley was sighted, but I was already committed to the short one! There was no power to make another approach. I retracted the gear and hit at the wrong end of the strip. The B-17 broke in half at the ball turret. We slid along at 100 mph and hit a pistol bunker on the left and a glider sling building on the right. The wingtips and the number four engine were torn off.

The B-17 barely slowed. An instant later we hit the railroad track and some power lines and slowed down considerably. The poor old airplane was by now completely on fire. All of the crew were rescued from the flames, but the plane was completely burned out when it came to rest in an apple orchard on the road to Emmen-Eschenbach.

Donald Waters, copilot 2LT William H. Conselman and engineer SGT Andrew Chianis were only slightly injured. The wreckage was later dismantled and taken to Dübendorf. The navigator, 1LT Alfred M. Shearer was killed in August of 1944 as he tried to climb up to his window in the Schweizerhof Hotel at Davos, slipped and fell, breaking his neck when he hit the ground.

1LT Charles S. Hardin's B-17G-35-DL (42-107137) was the other 100th BG ship that sought refuge in Switzerland that day. On this mission their usual navigator had been replaced by 2LT Thomas P. Hunt and the tail gunner S/SGT Robert J. Buchanan, was a spare from another crew. The ball turret gunner, S/SGT Norman D. Fuller, recalled the mission:

Because of the problem with our engines, we were not able to stay in the formation, and could not maintain altitude or speed. We dropped our bombs before reaching Munich and turned 180 degrees to head back to England. Almost immediately we received a direct flak hit and were badly crippled. We lost all fuel in the number three tank and this seriously limited our ability to stay airborne. As a result we took a heading to Switzerland. Very quickly, two Swiss fighters appeared and with a friendly dip of the wings motioned for us to follow them. They joined us on each wing and escorted us to the landing strip at Payerne.

Engineer S/SGT Norbert A. Fike added:

I dropped all gear, including the ball turret, and I was busy cranking down the landing gear due to failure of the hydraulic system. On landing we were greeted by soldiers pointing guns at us. We were questioned briefly and were housed overnight.

Harding's B-17G was the last Flying Fortress to leave Switzerland during October of 1945.

1LT Robert Turner's Natural Metal B-17G-35-DL (42-107031) Flying Fortress landed at Dübendorf with a feathered propeller on the number four engine. The engine was shut down because of flak damage. (Karl Hänggi)

CAHEPIT, a B-17G-1-BO (42-31074) of the 100th BG was completely demolished on a failed landing attempt at Emmen airfield. Luckily, none of 2LT Donald Waters' crew was injured in the crash. (F & W Emmen)

This B-26G crashed near Zuzgen on 16 April 1945. The pilot was killed, while the rest of the crew successfully bailed out.

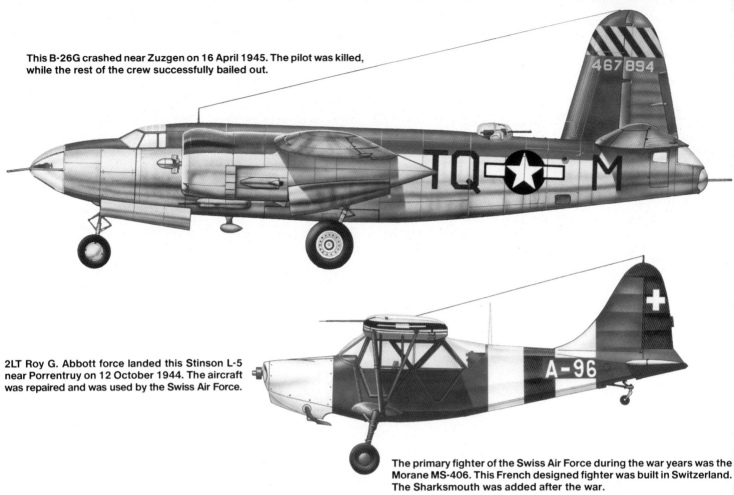

2LT Roy G. Abbott force landed this Stinson L-5 near Porrentruy on 12 October 1944. The aircraft was repaired and was used by the Swiss Air Force.

The primary fighter of the Swiss Air Force during the war years was the Morane MS-406. This French designed fighter was built in Switzerland. The Sharksmouth was added after the war.

The Messerschmitt Bf 109E-3 was also used by the Swiss Air Force to intercept and escort intruding aircraft. The Red/White neutrality markings were added after an incident where USAAF P-51s shot down two Swiss Bf-109Es.

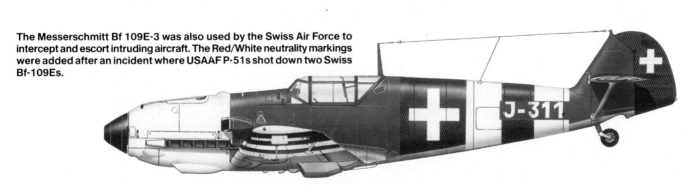

16 July 1944

On 16 July 1944, 1,087 bombers attacked Munich, Stuttgart, Augsburg and Saarbrücken. Eleven aircraft failed to return, one of which made it safely to Switzerland. This was the only aircraft reported as missing in action from the Stuttgart force.

The bomber was a B-17G-40-DL (44-6112) of the 385th BG flown by 1LT Norman V. Robbins, who had already accomplished more than 25 missions over Europe. The ship left the formation at 0916 with one propeller feathered and was given a fighter escort as it headed towards Switzerland.

1LT Norman V. Robbins' B-17G-40-DL (44-6112) had the number one engine feathered and the number three engine damaged by flak. It came to a sudden stop after the aircraft ground looped on landing, damaging the landing gear. (Karl Hänggi)

Before the aircraft entered Swiss airspace, it is believed German fighters attacked the ship. As they prepared for landing, the crew destroyed secret documents and materials. About 300 feet after touch down, the aircraft ground looped, destroying the right tire and the tail wheel, coming to rest another 240 feet down the runway. The right waist gunner, S/SGT Walter L. Cole, was slightly wounded and Swiss ground crews counted no less than seventeen shell holes in the aircraft. Additionally, the number three engine had been damaged from enemy action.

1LT Millard F. Pedigo's B-17G-30-BO (42-31889) suffered mechanical failure on two of its engines. The Olive Drab Fortress had previously flown with the 99th BG before its assignment to the 2nd BG. (Karl Hänggi)

18 July 1944

On 18 July 1944, the 15th Air Force attacked targets at Friedrichshafen and the Memmingen airfield. Friedrichshafen, located on the German side of Lake Constance, was quite close to Switzerland. None of the Friedrichshafen force landed in Switzerland; however, a single B-17 from the Memmingen force had to divert to Switzerland.

This event involved a lead crew from the 2nd Bomb Group, which was flying a rather old B-17G-30-BO (42-31889). The pilot, 1LT Millard F. Pedigo, had flown over thirty missions and had been selected for promotion to CAPT. The ship also carried the lead navigator, CAPT Mark O. Glasgow, and radio operator T/SGT William E. Aeschbacher, an enlisted man of Swiss descent, who recalled:

This B-17G-45-BO (42-97237) was landed at Dübendorf by 1LT Dick Mount with the number one engine feathered and the number three and four engines damaged by flak. The ball turret gunner, S/SGT. Frank V. Horetski, was killed. The aircraft had an Olive drab replacement tail gun position. (Fotohaus Wiesner)

I was with the 817th Squadron, 483rd Bomb Group and we flew to MacDill Field to begin our combat training on 1 November 1943. On 6 February 1944, we got our new airplane, a B-17G, serial 42-32031. Our Squadron CO wanted our ships named after Al Capps cartoon strip characters, so ours was named "MAMMY YOKUM" and this was painted on the ship.

We were transferred to the 2nd Bomb Group, 429th Squadron on 24 March 1944, and took "MAMMY YOKUM" with us. The ship was destroyed on 8 April 1944. We got back to our base but could not lower our landing gear and we crash landed with a full load of bombs. The plane was later used for repair parts. We were then assigned to ship 42-38078 and our crew had more time in this B-17 than any other, totalling thirty-nine sorties including the first shuttle mission to Russia. Our last mission was on 15 July 1944. We blew an engine and it was set to the depot for repair.

For the 18 July raid we were assigned a standby ship. There were only three of us on board from the original crew: the pilot, Millard Pedigo; right waist gunner S/SGT Paul L. Johnson; and myself. The beginning of our flight was uneventful, other than the fact we did not seem to have any fighter escort in our area. We pulled out of formation 10 to 15 minutes before the initial point when the number three and four engines began throwing oil. I think we were the fifth plane in our group to turn back. We salvoed our bombs, pulled out of formation and headed for home base. We threw everything we could overboard to lighten our load and when the number two engine began vibrating severely, our pilot told us to prepare for bailout.

With our predicament getting worse, chances were that we could not get back to our base, so we changed course and headed for Switzerland. Ten or fifteen minutes later, I heard over the intercom — "Look, coming in at 9 O'clock High, the Red Cross has sent us help. I did not know they had an Air Force." Sure enough there they were, three Swiss fighters who escorted us to fly to Dübendorf airfield. We landed with one good engine and were met with many armed Swiss soldiers. I did not know where we were for sure and at first I thought they might be German soldiers.

1LT Cyril J. Braund's B-17G-35-DL (42-107075) suffered a mid-air collision with another 91st BG Flying Fortress. The crew successfully bailed out and CHAMPAGNE GIRL crashed into a mountainside at Obersaxen, widely scattering the wreckage. (Karl Hänggi)

Three officers from CHAMPAGNE GIRL in the Davoser Hof pub in Davos. From left to right: copilot 2LT John Sykes, navigator 2LT Kenneth N. Bolz and the pilot, 1LT Cyril Braund. Kenneth Bolz spoke the Swiss-German language. (Cyril Braund)

19 July 1944

On 19 July 1944, the 8th and 15th Air Force launched a combined attack against industrial targets in southern and southwestern Germany. As a result, aircraft from both forces sought refuge in Switzerland. Two aircraft crashed, while three made safe landings.

1LT Cyril J. Braund flew his B-17G-35-DL (42-107075) of the 91st BG against Lechfeld. The Fortress was on its thirteenth mission and was called *Champagne Girl*, although the name was never painted on the bomber. About seven minutes before bombs away, the Fortress was caught in the prop wash of an aircraft ahead of it and slipped to the left. The wing tip hit the horizontal stabilizer of a B-17G (42-31542), named *BUNKY* and each aircraft pulled to the outside of the formation. The tail section of ship number 542 broke off and it spun down, crashing in Germany. Aircraft # 075 went into a flat spin, but the pilot managed to level off. The engineer, T/SGT Donald J. McBey, recalled:

> After that mid-air collision over the target we managed to keep the aircraft flying and headed for the Swiss border.

The pilot, Cyril Braund added:

> I, of course, was the last one to bailout and I had set the Fortress on auto-pilot, as best as the damage would allow. I watched it go down, with the wings level but in a steady decent. From my parachute, I watched it fly into the side of a mountain and explode. It was quite a sight!

The bomber crashed near the small town of Obersaxen, while the crew was picked up by Swiss guards between Ilanz and Castrisch. The wreckage of the ship was left in the inaccessable mountains after all the ammunition had been taken to the valley by a pair of pack horses.

ROYAL FLUSH II, a B-17G-45-BO (42-97237), had been attacked by enemy fighters shortly after the bomb run over the Linde Oxygen Factory at Höllkriegelskreuth near Munich. The pilot, 1LT Dick W. Mount, asked the Wing Commander permission to land in Switzerland, since he had four wounded men aboard and three engines were out. He then left the formation and headed for Switzerland. The German fighter attacks had slightly wounded the pilot who was on his tenth mission, but they instantly killed the ball turret gunner S/SGT Frank V. Horetski.

With only one good engine, Dick Mount managed to land at Dübendorf, where the three wounded crew members were immediately taken into the hospital. The Swiss recorded that three engines were damaged and counted forty-one holes in the aircraft.

Covered by a canvas cover from a Morane MS-406 fighter, Lt Simpson's P-51B-10-NA (42-106438) Mustang waits its check out by Swiss mechanics. The aircraft alongside it is a Bücker Bü 133 biplane trainer. (Martin Kyburz)

SLEEPY TIME GAL ran out of fuel and 2LT James V. Moran landed the B-24J-20-CF (42-99813) Liberator at Dübendorf. Ground crews prepare the bomber for the flight out of Switzerland to Burtonwood, England during the Summer of 1945. (A. Kistler)

The next aircraft to reach Switzerland was a P-51B-10-NA (42-106438) fighter which was on an escort mission for the Augsburg bomber force. The Mustang had been assigned to the 4th Fighter Group at Debden and was piloted by 1LT Curtis Simpson. The pilot recalls the mission:

> This particular escort flight was the sixth straight flight that we made to Munich in six days. We were jumped by a group of Messerschmitt Bf 109s and fought all the way into Austria. I had the aircraft on full throttle for too long a time and my electrical system on the coolant shutters went out. They closed and the engine overheated. I lost all my coolant and if I had not been so close to Switzerland I would have ended up as a POW or dead. God must have been riding with me. I was looking for a place to land the airplane, since I did not want to jump. I found this very short meadow that had some white signs on it so I thought I should try it. I had no other choice. I used full flaps with no power from the engine and I landed slightly on the tail wheel. There was no one there when I landed but as soon as I stopped the plane — here they came. The Swiss have helmets similar to the Germans and I was not sure where I was. I stood up in the cockpit with my hands raised and asked if they were Swiss; luckily they said yes.

The Mustang was a welcome addition to the Swiss Air Force inventory. Mechanics under the command of ADJ Urech dismantled the Mustang at the Ems-Plarenga airfield where the fighter landed. It was taken by trucks to the Chur railroad station and then by train to Dübendorf. The reassembled aircraft flew again for the first time with Swiss markings on 1 August 1944. Curtis Simpson escaped from Switzerland and returned to Debden on 15 October 1944.

JACK PINE JOE, a B-24H-15-FO (42-52466) of the 465th Bomb Group, was flown by 1LT Archie C. Davis on the mission to Munich. He already had twenty-one missions, including a trip to Ploesti five days earlier. The radio operator, S/SGT Alva H. Moss, recalled the flight:

> Over the target the number two engine went out and we could not feather the prop. Our navigator, 2LT Jackson C.

1LT Curtis Simpson of the 4th FG successfully landed his damaged P-51B-10-NA (42-106438) Mustang on the short grass runway at Ems-Plarenga airfield. The aircraft was later flown by the Swiss. (Swiss Air Force)

Johnson, bailed out and all the maps blew out the open hatch. Our pilot then headed for Switzerland. German fighters came alongside but did not make contact. We came too close to Friedrichshafen and got shot up. We crossed Lake Constance, then started leaving the airplane.

Unfortunately, the copilot, 2LT Michael W. Ballbach, was killed when he did not pull his rip cord. Three of the crew were injured and were taken to the hospital at Münsterlingen. The navigator, LT Johnson, who left the ship for unknown reasons, became a POW.

The pilotless *JACK PINE JOE* crashed into the castle of Wyden near Ossingen. This old castle ironically belonged to the President of the International Red Cross, Dr. H.C. Max Huber. The castle was heavily damaged from the impact and resulting fire.

The last landing of the day involved *SLEEPY TIME GAL*, a B-24J-20-CF (42-99813) of the 464th Bomb Group, flown by 2LT James V. Moran. Their mission had been to bomb the BMW-Works at Munich-Allach. The crew found themselves in trouble, when the superchargers failed, but Moran kept up with the formation and they dropped their bomb load over the target. A failure in the electrical system hampered the fuel transfer from the wing tanks to the main tanks, which meant that the aircraft would not make it back to Italy. West of Lienz in Austria, the bomber left the formation and headed for Switzerland where a safe landing was made at Dübendorf.

20 July 1944

On 20 July 1944, the 15th Air Force attacked Friedrichshafen on Lake Constance, right across the Swiss border, while the 8th Air Force attacked industrial targets in central Germany. Five Liberators from the 15th Air Force flew to Switzerland along with a single B-17G from the 8th Air Force.

The first aircraft was a B-24H-10-CF (42-64470) nicknamed *Rau Dee Dau*. The pilot, 1LT William E. Newhouse, recalled:

Mine was one of the original crews of the 747th Squadron, 456th Bomb Group that flew from the United States to Africa. Our squadron had consisted of seventeen crews. Of these original crews, we were the twelfth crew to be shot down and the last of the "old boys." Five crews were lucky enough to complete their tours and go home. This mission was our forty-second mission and we were to be sent home after fifty. The navigator, who was a replacement to my regular navigator, was on his 50th mission.

We received a burst of three rounds from some 88MM anti-aircraft guns, which disabled us. One hit in the bomb bay, one in the right wing fuel tank and the other in the number three engine. I was able to feather three engines, but the fourth was "running away." I was able to glide across Lake Constance and as soon as I saw that we were clear of the lake, I rang the bell to bailout. The crew landed in about a ten mile radius.

Vonnie Gal left Switzerland for Burtonwoodon, England on 25 September 1945. The aircraft still carried its nose art and combat scoreboard. Most of the B-17s that returned from Switzerland were scrapped in England. (Logan Muster)

2LT William Moore's B-17-F-75-DL (42-3524) shortly after it landed at Payerne airfield. The combat veteran was on its 50th mission when it was forced to divert to Switzerland. (Karl Hänggi)

Flown by the auto-pilot, the Liberator crashed on the Eggethof farm near Langrickenbach.

HELL'S BELLS, a B-24H-15-CO (42-52358) of the 459th BG, also became a victim of the heavy anti-aircraft defenses over the target. The Liberator was flown by 1LT Howland J. Hamlin and his copilot was 1LT Richard V. Newhouse, the cousin of William Newhouse, who piloted *Rau Dee Dau*.

At 1058, the ship peeled off from the formation and set course to Switzerland. Flak had virtually shot away the copilot's controls and a short time later gasoline was noticed spraying onto the flight deck. With the imminent hazard of a fire, the crew bailed out over Lake Constance. A shortly time later the Liberator exploded with most of the wreckage falling on German territory. Parts of the Liberator, including the tail, were found near Hemishofen in Switzerland.

The only man to actually land on Swiss soil was the engineer, T/SGT. Donald W. Anderson. The nose gunner, S/SGT Tommy Tonnessen, was rescued from Lake Constance by Swiss fishermen. The body of waist gunner S/SGT John A. Boardsen was later recovered from Lake Constance and buried at Münsingen.

The remaining six crew members either landed in the German part of Lake Constance itself or on the shore on the German side of the lake.

Several Swiss people, including the Mayor of Berlingen, had witnessed German troops across the lake firing on the crew as they parachuted to the ground. The same fishermen who rescued Tommy Tonnessen also attempted to rescue bombardier 1LT George T. Hunter, but were driven away by a German patrol boat. The bombardier was tangled in his parachute and drowned before the Germans could effect his rescue. This outrage was given considerable publicity by the Swiss newspapers and the local populace was greatly upset by this example of German barbarism.

Flak over the target also knocked out the 454th Bomb Group's lead ship, a B-24H-25-DT (42-51132) which was equipped with an H2X radar instead of the ball turret gun. The crew included the pilot, MAJ Franklin E. Tomlinson, copilot 1LT William Henry, lead navigator CAPT John J. Trautner, navigator 1LT John C. Schreck, radar navigator 1LT William A. Crews, bombardier CAPT. Edward E. Matthews, as well as five enlisted men.

One minute after bomb release, the Liberator feathered two engines and peeled off to the right of the formation and headed for Switzerland. The crew bailed out and the bomber crashed into a

Vonnie Gal **carried the 527th Bomb Squadron's unofficial squadron insignia between the unit identification letters. The Fortress was rather beat up with the skin covered with countless flak patches. (Karl Hänggi)**

small mountain near Weisslingen. The lead navigator, John J. Trautner, broke his ankle in the landing. MAJ Tomlinson became the Assistant Air Attache working in the American Legation in Berne.

2LT James Lester's B-24G-10-NT (42-78207) was having trouble with the oil pressure on the number one engine and the propeller was feathered about thirty minutes short of the target. The crew decided to turn back to base, but before they reached the Alps, the number three engine lost fuel pressure and failed. As a result the Liberator could not climb over the Alps and the crew decided to go to Switzerland. Shortly before the ship crossed the Swiss border, the number four engine began to run away; however, they were able to make a safe landing at Dübendorf.

2LT Jesse R. Furrow was flying a B-24G-10-NT (42-78197) of the 450th Bomb Group and his formation was among the first units to attack Friedrichshafen that day. The returning 450th BG crews reported that the flak was heavy and accurate. After bombs away, 2LT Furrow turned away from the formation and dropped down. Two pilots from other ship later stated that all four engines were operative and the ship under control.

Flying over Dübendorf airfield, the crew discovered that the elevator and rudders were not functioning and a landing under these conditions was out of the question. 2LT Furrow gave order to bailout and most of the men left the ship through the camera hatch. Unfortunately, the radio operator, S/SGT Charles D. Darragh, did not pull his rip cord and he was killed. He was buried at Münsingen two days later.

The pilotless bomber circled for about thirty minutes and after Jesse Furrow reported to the Swiss soldiers on the field that he was the last man out, Swiss fighters shot down the Liberator, which crashed near the town of Lindau in Canton Zurich. The Swiss were concerned that a shift in the wind might have caused the bomber to crash into the city of Winterthur.

2LT Howland J. Hamlin intended to bring his B-24H-15-FO (42-52358) to Switzerland. A fuel leak, however, forced the crew to bailout before the bomber exploded. Only a few parts of the Liberator fell on Swiss territory near Hemishofen and only two of the crew could be picked up by the Swiss. (Karl Hänggi)

53

The last aircraft to land participated in a raid against Leipzig and belonged to the 8th Air Force. This B-17F-75-DL (42-3524) named *Vonnie Gal* was the oldest operational aircraft of the 379th Bomb Group and was on its 50th mission. For most of these missions *Vonnie Gal* was flown by 1LT Jack LaMont and his crew had accomplished twenty-seven or twenty-eight missions in the Fortress. The Fortress had suffered serious damage on an earlier mission and had made it home with leaking fuel tanks and damaged engines. But on the 20 July mission, the Fortress' luck ran out. The aircraft was flown by 2LT William Moore who recalled the flight:

> We had just dropped our bombs over the target when we were hit by flak. We did not have full power, but were able to fly with one good engine. After we were out of range of the flak we were able to get the other engines going again, but we were losing fuel. Rather than having to ditch in the sea, my navigator, 1LT Jerry V. Barbar, gave me a heading for Switzerland. When we landed, we were not sure at first that we had made it to Switzerland, but luckily we had!

After the landing at Payerne airfield the crew was interrogated and then sent to two different places of internment.

Due to damage caused by anti-aircraft fire, the crew abandoned *Rau Dee Dau* and the B-24 crashed near Langrickenbach. (W.E. Newhouse)

2LT James Lester's B-24G-10-NT (42-78207) named *The Wikie*, was the only 15th Air Force aircraft that actually landed on 20 July 1944. The aircraft had the number one engine shut down and feathered, but no other damage was found by the Swiss. (Fotohaus Wiesner)

21 July 1944

On 21 July 1944, the 8th Air Force sent a force of 1,110 bombers into southern Germany and Bavaria. By end of the day, the 8th AF had lost thirty-one aircraft, twenty-two of which were from the 2nd Air Division. Eight Liberators sought refuge in Switzerland.

The only 3rd Air Division Liberator that landed in Switzerland was the first to land that day. The B-24H-20-FO (42-94821) belonged to the 490th Bomb Group, which had lost only two Liberators in forty missions. Named *PETE THE PELICAN*, the ship was assigned to 2LT James R. Smith and his crew, who were on their second mission.

On the way to the target, the number one and four engines had to be shut down because of a loss of oil pressure. Smith informed the lead pilot that he was going to try for Switzerland. With reduced power, the ship lost a lot of altitude and the crew threw everything possible out of the aircraft to lighten the Liberator. Shortly before they reached the Swiss border, German flak fired on the aircraft.

A Swiss C-36 multi-purpose aircraft guided the ship to Dübendorf and shortly after touchdown, the nosewheel collapsed and the entire nose section broke away.

The 492nd BG was not spared a loss on this mission. 1LT William M. Walker was flying a B-24J-155-CO (44-40290), a replacement aircraft which already had flown twenty-three missions, when he began having trouble with the number four and number three engines. Additionally, the gunner reported that the tail turret was inoperative. The higher power setting on the remaining engines resulted in a higher fuel consumption, which meant that the Liberator could not return to base. As a result, 1LT Walker jettisoned the bombs and headed for Switzerland. He was escorted by Swiss fighters to Dübendorf.

2LT James F. Beaver was flying *LITTLE SHEPPARD*, a B-24H-10-DT (41-28711), to Munich-Allach. On the way back from the target, they lost three engines and the crew diverted to Switzerland. Unfortunately, the landing at Dübendorf was too fast and the ship skidded into a cornfield, where the nosewheel broke.

1LT Stanley V. Scott was flying a B-24H-25-FO (42-95218) on the way to Kempten. Shortly after leaving the target area, Scott's ship

CHANNEL HOPPER parked on its hardstand at its home base prior to a mission. This B-24H-25-FO (42-95226) of the 44th Bomb Group would later end up interned in Switzerland. (Tony North)

LITTLE SHEPPARD, a B-24H-10-DT (41-28711) Liberator, was flown by 2LT James F. Beaver. The aircraft overran the runway and came to a halt in a nearby cornfield. Both the number one and number three engines were shut down and the propellers were feathered. (Karl Hänggi)

was hit by flak in the number two engine, which began to burn. He dropped out of formation and was escorted by nine P-38s to the Swiss border. After crossing the Swiss border, one Swiss anti-aircraft unit shot at the aircraft, but did not score a hit. Swiss fighters finally guided the Liberator to Dübendorf.

The 389th BG had been briefed to bomb the marshalling yards at Saarbrücken and among this force was *GINNY GAL*, A B-24H-25-FO (42-95077) piloted by 1LT Key R. Caldwell. About thirty minutes short of the target, the number one engine overheated and had to be feathered. A few minutes later, the same thing happened with the number four engine. The crew headed for Switzerland, but on landing the aircraft overran the field and crashed into an anti-aircraft

Ginny Gal, a B-24H-25-FO (42-95077) Liberator, overran the runway and crashed into a camouflaged anti-aircraft gun site. The entire nose section was destroyed, but none of 1LT Kay R. Caldwell's crew was seriously injured. (Fotohaus Wiesner)

The nosewheel collapsed as F/O Donald F. Tofte overran the runway. The B-24H-25-FO (42-95226) Liberator carried no ball turret. *CHANNEL HOPPER* arrived in Switzerland because of a supercharger failure on the number three engine. (Swiss Air Force)

2LT Stanley V. Scott arrived at Dübendorf with the number four engine shut down and feathered. His B-24H-25-FO (42-95218) Liberator was returned to England carrying a new number one engine taken from a Liberator with a Black cowling. (Fotohaus Wiesner)

PETE THE PELICAN, a B-24 H-20-FO (42-94821), crash landed with both the number one and number four engines feathered. 2LT James R. Smith overran the runway and the nose section was broken way from the rest of the fuselage when the nosegear collapsed. (Karl Hänggi)

gun site on the airfield boundary at Dübendorf. The crash destroyed the entire nose section of *GINNY GAL* but none of the crew was seriously injured.

F/O Donald F. Tofte's B-24H-25-FO (42-95226) had been damaged by flak over the target. The *Channel Hopper* had lost the supercharger on the number three engine and a fuel line had been cut. With the loss of fuel, a safe return to England was impossible. After crossing the Swiss border, Swiss anti-aircraft guns shot at the Liberator, but missed. Morane fighters escorted the plane to Dübendorf, but the Liberator overran the runway and ended up in a cornfield with a broken nosewheel.

1LT John R. Anderson and crew were flying a rather notorious 44th BG aircraft, the *MARY HARRIET*, a replacement B-24J-130-CO (42-110049) which had been transferred to the 44th by the 453rd Bomb Group. It was well known in the group because of its maintenance problems. The ship performed so badly that even with four engines running it was difficult to hold in formation.

Flak over the target was very heavy and accurate and knocked out one engine. Anderson decided to fly to the nearest safe place and asked the navigator, 2LT James A. Hewlett, for a heading to Switzerland. Unfortunately, the navigator had forgotten his maps of Switzerland and navigation became difficult, since part of Switzerland, including Lake Constance, was covered by clouds.

For over an hour the crew tried to find Dübendorf airfield but

couldn't and no Swiss fighters came up to escort them to safety. *MARY HARRIET* was over the Canton of Appenzell at an altitude of 6,000 feet, far to the east of Dübendorf and, as the fuel ran out, LT Anderson gave the order to bailout. Unfortunately, the left waist gunner's (S/SGT Leo J. Hoffman) parachute failed to open and he was killed. The other crew members safely reached Swiss soil and were taken to the Hotel Krone in Appenzell and then to Dübendorf. The pilotless Liberator headed for mount Schwägalp and finally crashed above the small town of Nesslau.

The last landing of the day was made by another 492nd Bomb Group Liberator. The B-24J-55CF (44-10496) arrived as a replacement and was on its second mission with the 492nd Bomb Group. The bomber was flown by 2LT William H. Wesson and on this mission they carried no bombardier. Anti-aircraft fire damaged the number three engine which had to be feathered. Additionally, the oil tank on the number two engine was also hit resulting in the loss of all oil pressure in the engine and one of the crew was injured. On top of all these troubles, a fire broke out in the bomb bay which was successfully extinguished by the crew. At 1000, in the vicinity of Mannheim, Wesson contacted the lead, CAPT Graham, and told him that he was going to try for Switzerland.

The Navigator, F/O Roger W. Buckholz, found Dübendorf and they made a safe landing. The Swiss noted that there was no ball turret fitted to the Liberator and they counted no less than thirty shell holes in the aircraft.

2LT William H. Wesson's B-24J-55-CF (44-10496) landed with the number three engine shut down and feathered and the number two engine losing oil. During the Summer of 1945, the Swiss repaired the aircraft and painted out the national markings. (Weltwoche Bilderarchiv)

1LT John R. Anderson's crew had to bailout from their B-24J-130-CO (42-110049) Liberator after it ran out of fuel. The crew was taken to the Hotel Krone in Appenzell where they were given their first Swiss meal. (James A. Hewlett)

31 July 1944

On 31 July 1944, the 1st and 3rd Air Division were sent to Munich, Munich-Allach and Schleissheim. Of the 705 aircraft that went on the mission, ten were reported as missing in action, although two of them made it safely to Dübendorf airfield.

2LT Victor L. Lewis flew to the target in a B-17G-25-DL (42-38034) named *TWAT'S IT TO YOU*. The first problem occurred over the target when only two of the five bombs could be dropped. The rest were jettisoned manually after leaving the target. The flak over the target was very heavy and accurate. The Fortress was hit in the number four engine which had to be feathered. The number one engine was also out of action because of a loss of oil pressure. With only two good engines, there was little hope in reaching England and the navigator, F/O Edward Whiston, gave the pilots a heading to Switzerland. Shortly after crossing the border, Swiss fighters picked up the B-17G and guided it to Dübendorf where it made a safe landing.

The next aircraft to land was the only aircraft from the 401st Bomb Group to be interned in Switzerland. The B-17G-35-DL (42-107092) was flown by 2LT Jay D. Ossiander. His engineer, S/SGT Penrose W. Reagan, recalled the mission:

Our Fortress actually had two names: the other name was FRECKLES, which was a Rita Hayworth type girl in a bathing suit, while a large head of Jimmy Durante was painted on the copilot's side. We blew a tail wheel on takeoff, which was the start of our problems. After we turned on to the IP, the number two engine began throwing oil and our pilot, Jay Ossiander, instead of dropping our bombs and going around the target and picking up the group on the way home, decided to take us across the target through heavy flak with three engines.

The number two propeller would not feather and kept going back into high pitch. As a result, the number two engine lost all of its oil and seized. The propeller continued to rotate, stripping the propeller reduction gears, allowing the propeller to rotate freely which caused considerable vibration.

By this time we had dropped out of the group and became a straggler, while the group went on to bomb the target. We had been flying the last ship, low squadron, commonly known as the Purple Heart Corner. As we went over the target and into the flak area, we were hit again in the number three engine which started throwing oil. The pilot by this time decided not to proceed through the target area and we salvoed our bombs and made a banking turn to the left. As we made the bank, two rockets went by on the right side from 6 o'clock low to 12 o'clock high. If we had not made the bank, we would have been hit by the rockets.

About 400 yards off to our right a B-17 exploded and no parachutes were seen. This ship was not from our bomb group and like ourselves, was a straggler. The propeller on the number three engine duplicated the same sequence of events as had the number two engine. By this time we were having difficulty maintaining altitude because two of the propellers were frozen in the high pitch position creating a lot of drag. Additionally there was a lot of severe vibration set up by the two windmilling props.

2LT Jay Ossiander's B-17G-35-DL (42-107092) Fortress had the gear box on the number one damaged and the number three engine was leaking oil. The nose art is the head of Jimmy Durante, which was carried only on the starboard side. (Karl Hänggi)

The number one and four engines were boosted to emergency power ratings; however, the number four engine started to overheat and we had to reduce the power setting of that engine. By this time it was quite clear we were not going to make it to England, which is where we had intended to go after coming off the target. As our situation deteriorated, we set a course for Yugoslavia. It soon became obvious that this too could not be reached and we then set course for Switzerland.

By now we were 1,200 to 1,500 feet off the deck. Someone called, "ME-109s at 9 O'clock!" I popped back into the upper turret and swung my guns on them. At this time the closest 109 flipped its wings up so we could see the Swiss cross, then it proceeded to drop his wheels and motioned for us to follow him. The fighters took us to Dübendorf airfield. It was then that we found out one of our main landing gear tires had been shot out. This tire, plus the tail wheel tire that had blown on takeoff made the landing a bit dicey, since the aircraft wanted to ground loop. However, control was maintained and the powers that be, smiled on us again.

After interrogation, the two crews were held overnight in the Officers' Casino at Dübendorf. These buildings were under guard by Swiss soldiers, but Jay Ossiander, the pilot on UMBRIAGO/ FRECKLES managed to escape and buy a train ticket at the Dübendorf train station. He was finally caught at the Berne main station that same night, calmly waiting for a train to Geneva.

TWAT'S IT TO YOU **was a B-17G-25-DL (42-38034) Flying Fortress flown by 2LT Victor L. Lewis. He brought the B-17 to Switzerland with the number one engine damaged and the number four engine out and the propeller feathered. (Karl Hänggi)**

August Arrivals

During August of 1944 only three 15th and one 8th Air Force aircraft landed in Switzerland. On 3 August, the 15th flew a raid to Friedrichshafen, which resulted in two aircraft diverting to Switzerland.

Aircraft 39, a B-24G-17-NT (42-78439) of the 484th Bomb Group was flown by 2LT Harry Schultz. Shortly before the formation reached the IP over Bregenz, the Liberator's oxygen system failed. At 1048, the pilot left the formation and dropped down to 9,000 feet so the crew could breath. Since there were still strong enemy fighter forces operating in northern Italy, the crew decided to divert to Switzerland rather face the probability of being shot down as a straggler. The pilot brought the Liberator in for a safe landing at Dübendorf, even though the bomber carried a full bomb load of nine 500 pound bombs.

2LT James E. Heintz and his crew flew a B-17G-25-BO (42-31655) against Oberraderach near Friedrichshafen. This chemical plant produced fuel for the V.2 rocket. The copilot, 2LT George W. Eilers, was not the regular copilot and the of bombardier, 2LT Jacob R. Blumer, was of Swiss descent.

The formation ran into heavy anti-aircraft fire over the target and the Fortress was hit in the number one engine, which could not be feathered. The windmilling propeller produced a lot of drag and vibration. Additionally, the oxygen line to the tail gunner, S/SGT Joseph Ferreira, was cut.

2LT Heintz called the Group leader, LTCOL John D. Ryan, and told him that he could not make it back to Italy and was going into Switzerland. Shortly after crossing the Swiss border, a number of anti-aircraft guns fired on them. Heinz immediately lowered the landing gear as a sign of surrender and began to fire flares. The AA fire stopped after thirty seconds. The navigator, 2LT James F. Mahon, found Dübendorf without the aid of a Swiss fighter escort, but the landing was too fast and the B-17 overran the airfield boundary and crossed the main street of Dübendorf-Uster. The landing gear was ripped off and the aircraft skidded to a halt on its belly, damaging

STRUGGLE BUGGY, a B-24H-15-FO (42-94785) Liberator flown by 1LT Maynard Kisinger was hit by flak in the left main fuel tank. The loss of fuel led the crew to divert to Switzerland. (Fotohaus Wiesner)

2Lt Harry Schultz flew this B-24G-17-NT (42-78439) to Switzerland when the oxygen system failed. Stripped of its national markings and tactical numbers, the Liberator was used to conduct a demonstration flight for GEN Legge, the U.S. Military Attache, and high ranking Swiss officers on 8 August 1944. (Fotohaus Wiesner)

When not in use, the engines and cockpit were covered with canvas covers. LT Schultz's B-24G-17-NT (42-78439) was later placed in open storage at Dübendorf airfield along with many other B-17s and B-24s. (Weltwoche Bilderarchiv)

A Swiss-built C-36 multi-purpose aircraft escorts this B-24J-195-CO (44-41121) Liberator of the 465th Bomb Group to Dübendorf airfield. The bomber had the number four engine shut down and the propeller was feathered. (Fotohaus Wiesner)

2LT Howard Secors B-24J-195-CO (44-41121) had the port landing gear leg collapse after a hard landing. The number four engine has a feathered propeller and the number one engine was ripped from the wing during the crash landing. (Fotohaus Wiesnenr)

the entire front section of the aircraft. Fortunately, none of the crew was seriously hurt in the crash landing.

On 11 August 1944, sixty 2nd Air Division Liberators attacked the marshalling yards at Saarbrücken. The 489th Bomb Group sent out thirty-eight B-24s and the outfit's only loss, *STRUGGLE BUGGY*, a B-24H-15-FO (42-94785) was lucky enough to reach Switzerland. The Liberator was flown by 1LT Maynard W. Kisinger and on this mission the crew had no navigator. The radio operator T/SGT Albert P. Hall recalled:

We were hit by flak and lost two engines and most of our fuel. We knew we could not make it back to England so we headed for Switzerland. We were contacted by a Swiss fighter and directed to an airport, where we landed in accordance with procedures that had been covered in a number previous briefings before the mission. All secret info was destroyed before we landed.

After the landing at Dübendorf, the Swiss noted that *STRUGGLE BUGGY* did not carry a ball turret and there were three flak holes in fuselage and in the right wing.

On 16 August 1944, the 15th Air Force went after strategic targets at Friedrichshafen and the V.2 fuel plant at Oberraderach. German defenses caused damage to one Liberator that made a safe landing, while another was so badly damaged that the crew bailed out over Switzerland. CAPT Lewis M. Robert's B-24H-15-DT (41-28904) had been damaged over the target. Roberts had led the 465th Bomb Group to Oberraderach as a lead ship carrying two navigators, 1LT Elliott B. Sweet and 2LT Donald A. Barrett. The regular bombardier was 1LT James J. Lyons, and, since the Liberator carried H2X radar, the crew included a radar navigator/bombardier, 2LT Richard A. Burgin.

With a fuel leak, the Liberator left the formation with an escort of four P-51s and headed toward Switzerland. The crew bailed out and the eleven Americans landed at Stein an Rhine on the Rhine river very close to the German border. The Liberator, flying on auto-pilot, headed back into Germany, where it crashed.

2LT Howard Secor's B-24J-15-CO (44-41121) was another victim of the heavy and accurate flak over the target area. The number four engine lost oil pressure and had to be feathered, while the number one engine could not be feathered and was windmilling. This led the pilot to make a decision to leave the formation and head for Switzerland.

The stricken bomber was picked up by a Swiss C-36 multipurpose aircraft and escorted to Dübendorf. 2LT Secor landed long and hard, breaking the left main landing gear leg. The port wingtip hit the ground, causing considerable damage including a number of bent propeller blades. The ship, because of its damage, was dismantled and scrapped after the war.

2LT James E. Heintz overran the runway and as the B-17G-25-BO (42-31655) crossed the main street of Dübendorf - Uster, the landing gear was sheered off. The 2nd BG Group marking was applied on the vertical fin and on the horizontal stabilizer. (Karl Hänggi)

September Arrivals

Nine aircraft landed during September of 1944. On 5 September 1944, the 8th Air Force went to Stuttgard, Ludwigshafen and Karlsruhe; of the 739 bombers on these missions, only six failed to return and two of these landed in Switzerland.

The first aircraft was a B-24H-25-FO (42-95205), named by the crew *The Lonesome Polecat*. The pilot, 1LT John V. Fanelli, recalled the mission:

The plane had been named by the ground crew chief, SGT Joseph Porter, because the flight crew was bickering over the name. He named it "The Lonesome Polecat" and when asked why he had picked that name, he said, "This ship is on the ground more often than any of the others. It is always having shrapnel and bullet holes repaired. It sits here like a lonesome polecat," and that's how it got the name.

Ths bombardier, 2LT William Baxter was freshly arrived in the European theater and was on his first orientation flight with my crew. Flight officer John R. Greim was our navigator and the baby of the crew. He was just over eighteen years old. We almost lost LT Baxter south of Karlsruhe after we had been flipped over on our back, burning and out of control. Fifteen thousand feet down I brought it back under control. LT Baxter had made a dash for the open bomb bay door but was stopped by our radio man SGT John Tharpe.

The bomber landed at Dübendorf and investigation by the Swiss showed that the number one engine had overheated and shrapnel had hit the oil tank behind the number four engine.

The circumstances under which *BLUES IN THE NIGHT*, a B-17G-70-BO (43-37866) landed were quite tragic for the Swiss. CAPT Alvin W. Jaspers, as command pilot had led the 390th Bomb Group to the Daimler-Benz Factory at Stuttgart, flying in the copilot's seat beside the pilot, 1LT Thomas E. Gallagher. Instead of an enlisted man, 2LT Walter L. Underwood acted as tail gunner and observer. The navigator, 2LT Daniel Foley told about the mission:

This B-17G-70-BO (43-37866) was a lead ship and carried command pilot CAPT Alvin W. Jaspers. They landed in Switzerland with the number one and number four engines shut down and feathered. The crew of *BLUES IN THE NIGHT* jettisoned the ball turret before landing. (Fotohaus Wiesner)

Oberleutnant R. Heiniger bellied in his badly damaged Messerschmitt Bf 109E-3, side number J-324, at Dübendorf airfield after he was attacked twice by 339th Fighter Group P-51 Mustangs. (Fotohaus Wiesner)

Just after bombs away we turned sharply to the right and dropped a thousand feet to 24,000 feet. I looked back and saw Horton and Strate, our number two and three men catching hell in the flak. I was feeling kind of sorry for them when Gallagher feathered our number four engine. Number two was running rough and smoking, and number three had a fuel leak. By then our number one engine had to be feathered too, and I began to doubt our ability to return to Framlingham. Ball turret gunner S/SGT James B. Eckman called up from the turret in his regular damage assessment report and said that oil was pouring from the number two engine and that the number one, three and four fuel tanks were holed. I was nevertheless surprised to hear CAPT Jaspers surrender the group lead to our deputy, Evans.

We made the only choice possible and decided to try and reach Switzerland. I realized with a sickening feeling that I had no navigation charts south of 48 degrees latitude! Although I have since realized that our emergency map in the escape kit contained a general chart of the area. Of course it was obvious that the lake off to the left was Constance, and since it was general knowledge among Eight Air Force Navigators that the Friedrichshafen flak area extended over a portion of the lake, we skirted the western end of the water.

As we approached, four Mustangs joined us as escorts — a welcome sight indeed! As I remembered the general layout, Zürich was at the head of a long, narrow lake southwest of Bodensee. We had just crossed the Rhine into Switzerland near Schaffhausen when Victor H. Estes saw a large city to the southwest and a couple of moments later, he spotted the long, arrow lake as well. We altered course to about 250 degrees and made for the city. Shortly afterwards we received a few wild bursts of anti-aircraft fire from a small town we later learned was Frauenfeld. To my mind, Frauenfeld is very significant, since that was my last experience with flak during World War II.

THE LONESOME POLECAT was a B-24H-25-FO (42-95205) Liberator flown by 1st Lt John V. Fanelli. The aircraft was not named by the aircrew. The ground crew chief named the aircraft after the crew could not decide on a name. (Fotohaus Wiesner)

2LT Robert W. Kaub's B-17G Flying Fortress was damaged by flak over Czechoslovakia. The crew of *HOLEY JOE* removed everything that was not necessary and jettisoned it in order to lighten the B-17G-30-BO (42-31834) before landing. (Fotohaus Wieser)

CAPT Jaspers did not think we were in Swiss air space in spite of my assurances and consequently he had not notified the high flying Mustangs when we crossed the Rhine. Two Swiss fighters that had come to meet us were shot down by the Mustangs in one pass. The American fighters then went down to strafe the field and belatedly discovered that they were in Switzerland.

In a desperate effort to lighten the ship, we had thrown flak suits, guns, and even the ball turret out of the aircraft. When it became apparent that we were out of Germany we tossed our radar material into the water as we flew over the lake. We later learned that the 1,800 pound ball turret had fallen through the upper three stories of a building, but fortunately nobody was hurt. Gallagher saw the field was a bit damp, and we slid in, skidding to a stop at the very end of the 1,800 foot dirt field.

1LT Earl E. Erickson and 2LT Nathan Ostrow of the 339th Fighter Group attacked the two Messerschmitt Bf 109E which had arrived to escort the bomber to Dübendorf, in the first pass Oberleutnant Paul Treu, flying J-378 was killed and his aircraft crashed near Neuaffoltern.

Oberleutnant Robert Heiniger, flying J-324, was attacked by the other Mustangs but managed to belly in his fatally stricken fighter at Dübendorf. Both pilots belonged to *Fliegerkompanie 7*. 2LT Nathan Ostrow was credited with 1.5 kills that day, while 1LT Earl E. Erickson was credited with half a victory, but on 11 September 1944 he was credited with another victory - this time a real German aircraft!

CAPT William C. Riddel and his crew ran into trouble on the way to the Lechfeld on 12 September 1944. At 1310 the B-24H-20-DT (41-28989) left formation over Donauwörth and headed, with fighter protection, for Switzerland. Due to a mechanical failure the number three engine overheated and failed. Additionally, a fuel shortage made a safe return to San Giovanni impossible. Without further incident *Reddy Teddy Too* landed at Dübendorf. Apart from the defective engines, no other damage was reported by the Swiss.

CHATTANOOGA CHOO CHOO was 2LT Theodore H. Bowling's B-24H-20-DT (41-28994) Liberator. The aircraft landed in Switzerland with two engines out and the props feathered and with the number four engine losing oil. (Fotohaus Wiesner)

Lines of parked American bombers on the grass at Dübendorf airfield. The aircraft in the foreground was 2LT Richard A. Huber's B-24J-15-CF (42-99748). The Liberator was being overhauled during the Summer of 1945 in front of the Swissair hangar. (Fotohaus Wiesner)

2LT Richard A. Huber's B-24J-15-CF (42-99748) was another 455th Bomb Group Liberator that did not make it back to Italy. A mechanical failure in the number one engine led to it being feathered and the number two engine also began to malfunction. South of the initial point on the run to Lechfeld air base, the ship jettisoned its bomb load and headed for Switzerland. At 1340, they made a safe landing at Dübendorf.

CHATTANOOG CHOO CHOO was the last 455th Bomb Group Liberator to land that day. The B-24H-20-DT (41-28994) was flown by 2LT Theodore H. Bowling and with seventy-two combat missions, the plane was a veteran. Enemy fighters attacked the ship and damaged three of the engines as well as the fuel tanks. There was very little choice for the crew of *CHATTANOOGA CHOO CHOO* and they decided to set course for Switzerland. Before landing, the left waist gun was dropped. At 1408 they made a safe landing at Payerne with only 237 gallons of fuel left! Swiss ground crews counted no less than twenty-three machine gun and three cannon holes in the Liberator.

On 13 September 1944, the 8th Air Force sent 1,026 bombers against oil and industrial targets in southern Germany. Fifteen aircraft were reported as MIA and only one made it safely to Switzerland. The 92nd BG failed to bomb its primary and headed for Altenburg. Over the target, *HEAVENS ABOVE*, a B-17G-35-BO (42-31995) lost one engine. The Fortress was on its last mission and was flown by 2LT Warren D. Stallings, who took the Flying Fortress to Switzerland, where a safe landing was made at Dübendorf.

On 22 September 1944, the 15th Air Force attacked Munich and two Liberators sought refuge in neutral Switzerland.

FLYING, a B-24H-25-CF (42-50404) of the 465th BG, had suffered damage to the tail section on a previous mission and to make repairs on the Liberator, the maintenance chief "borrowed" the left fin and rudder from aircraft 42-78108, and this serial number was still stenciled on the fin when they took off from Pantanella with 2LT Roger L. Kraft at the controls.

CAPT William C. Riddel's B-24H-20-DT (41-28989) was on its fifty-first mission when it diverted to Switzerland. The last three digits of the serial number were repeated on the nose in Black and the name *REDDY TEDDY TOO* was carried on the starboard side of the Liberator. (Karl Hänggi)

2LT William J. Kristen landed at Dübendorf with one engine feathered and another losing oil. *NAUGHTY NAN* was a B-24H-21-DT (41-28997) and it had a second name, *BROOKLYN*, which was written on the cowling of the number one engine. (Karl Hänggi)

2LT Roger L. Kraft belly landed his B-24H-25-CF (42-50404) at Altenrhein with the number one engine shut down and three other engines losing oil. *FLYING* had a replacement port fin and rudder from another B-24 (serial 42-78108) and went into combat with that serial number still painted on the fin. (Karl Hänggi)

FLYING ran into strong German anti-aircraft fire and lost oil pressure on three engines while the fourth engine had to be feathered. The ship barely limped into Swiss airspace. The landing gear was jammed and 2LT Kraft had to belly land the B-24, which was a difficult undertaking. After skidding for some 900 feet, *FLYING* finally came to rest at Altenrhein. None of the crew was injured in the belly landing and Swiss ground crews found some thirty holes in the Liberator. The bomber was dismantled and shipped to Kloten for storage.

2LT William J. Kristen flew B-24H-21-DT (41-28997) to Bavaria. In addition to the regular crew the Liberator had a photographer, CPL William E. Close, on board. During the bomb run, the ship was hit by flak in the bomb bay and in the engines and a fire broke out in the bomb bay. At 1256, *NAUGHTY NAN* pulled out of formation and headed towards Switzerland. There was a big hole in the number one fuel tank, the number one engine had to be feathered and number three had lost a lot of oil. With the fuel nearly gone, *NAUGHTY NAN* crossed the border and was escorted by Moranes of *Fliegerkompagnie* 13 to Dübendorf. On landing there was less than 220 gallons of fuel remaining in the Liberator's tanks.

On 23 September, 504 B-17s of the 15th Air Force bombed the Sudetenländische Treibstoffwerke (Syntetic Oil Production Plant) at Brüx, Czechoslovakia. Only two aircraft were reported as missing in action and one landed in Switzerland. *HOLEY JOE*, a B-17G-30-BO (42-31834) of the 463rd BG, flown by 2LT Robert W. Kaub, suffered supercharger trouble short of the IP. After bombs away, 2LT Kaub called the group leader and told him that they would try to reach an emergency landing field in friendly territory.

But the crew was soon plagued with more trouble. The oxygen system failed, and the instruments went out. A decision was made to head for Switzerland and the crew began to throw out anything removable in order to lighten the ship, including all the guns and the ball turret. At 1,000 feet AGL, the Fortress crossed the border and was met by Moranes of *Fliegerkompagnie* 13. On the final approach to Dübendorf, the pilot found that the port landing gear could not be lowered, either normally or manually. After making another pass, 2LT Kaub bellied in *HOLEY JOE*. Luckily, no on in the crew was injured in the crash landing.

This Red tailed B-17G-35-BO (42-31995), flown by 2LT Warren D. Stallings, landed at Dübendorf with a damaged number four engine. The high visibility Red tail band had been introduced during the Summer of 1944. (Karl Hänggi)

Fall 1944

From October to December of 1944, only seven American aircraft were interned in Switzerland.

On 4 October 1944, the 15th Air Force once again bombed Munich. 1LT Samuel B. Peskin of the 464th Bomb Group was flying *Brown Nose*, a B-24H-15-FO (42-52485). The flight engineer, T/SGT Joseph Z. Krajewski, recalled the mission:

After formation assembly, we headed for Munich. We had to face heavy and accurate flak and were hit by four close bursts. The bomb bay doors had just been opened when we were hit. I was sitting on the radio operator's stool behind copilot LT Frank Hoch when he was knocked out of his seat. I was hit above my right eyebow by a piece of flak and the blood ran down my face. Both hydraulic accumulators burst and caught fire, but they were quickly extinguished. The navigator, 2LT Earl Thompson pulled the emergency handle to the front wheel doors so we would be able to jump if necessary. The flak cut a hole on the right side of the ship from the nose to the bomb bay under the right wing. The second burst, above the ship, knocked the front turret gunner, SGT Louis E. Loftiss, out of his turret, and hit the bombardier, LT Kyle Abernathy, in the right arm.

At this time, three engines cut out and we started to dive. The copilot, Frank Hoch, was on the floor unconscious, so I jumped into his seat and helped the pilot, Sam Peskin, fight the controls. The plane dropped in a steep glide from 21,000 feet to 14,000 feet, when two engines restarted and for a split second pulled 60

Swiss anti-aircraft fire knocked out a fuel line forcing 2LT Roy G. Abbot to land his Stinson L-5-WV (42-99186) Sentinel at Vacherie. The aircraft was taken to Dübendorf where it was repaired. (Fotohaus Wiesner)

This 50th Fighter Group P-47D-22-RE (42-26063) Thunderbolt was shot down by Swiss Messerschmitt Bf 109E3 fighters. While attempting to land it was also hit by Swiss flak. Although damaged, 2LT Jerald Conlan made a good belly landing at Laufen. (Karl Hänggi)

inches of manifold pressure (30 inches normal) until LT Peskin pulled back on the throttles and readjusted the controls. The number three engine never restarted, since the shell had damaged the engine and wing tank. Gas leaked into the bomb bay area and was being blown around. After we regained stability on the three engines, the copilot regained consciousness and returned to his seat. I had to release the ten 500 pound bombs with a screw driver, since the bomb toggle control had been hit and the intercom was out.

The radio operator S/SGT Ray Menzl, who was manning the right waist gun, had been hit in the left leg. I had to transfer gas from the Tokyo outer tanks to the inner main tanks which were over the front bomb bay. Then I returned to the waist compartment. The tail gunner SGT Norman Gibbard, told me that LT Peskin wanted me up on the flight deck. The waist right side had also been hit by a burst of flak.

The pilot asked the navigator, 1LT William Thompson, to chart a course for France since we kept losing altitude and gas and would not be able to fly over the Alps back to home base. Heading west, we were fired on by anti-aircraft fire near Friedrichshafen but we were not hit. The navigator and bombardier bandaged the unconscious nose turret gunner, Louis Loftiss', head not knowing that he had been hit in the arm and shoulder as well.

We started to throw out all unnecessary and loose articles out of the bomb bay as well as the guns, ammunition, extra clothing, bomb sight, anything we could get our hands on to lighten the load.

The top turret gunner, SGT Michael D. Mitchell, called down that two planes were heading towards us and that the silhouettes were Me 109s. With that I loaded the very pistol and started to shoot up a distress signal (flares) hoping this would not blow all us up and to let the fighters understand that we were disabled.

When the fighters were alongside, they tipped up their wings to show their markings which were a White cross on a Red background — Swiss. Boy were we overjoyed. We could not communicate because the radio was out. But Sam gave them a "thumbs up" and we followed them to Dübendorf. We could not land until I lowered the main landing gear manually.

After circling the field three times, the two pilots in the Me 109s became upset because we did not land. We finally started to align for landing and came in at 170 miles an hour (normal is 125 mph), since we had no control over the flaps and no brakes. There was a deep drainage ditch at the end of the runway which sheared off the nosewheel. The ship stopped only fifteen feet short of the trees at the other side of the drainage ditch.

The seriously wounded crew members were taken to the hospital and there were more than 100 flak holes in the skin of *BROWN NOSE*.

On 12 October 1944, 2LT Roy G. Abbott and his passenger were flying a Stinson L-5-WV (42-99186) on a liaison flight for the 324th FG, a 12th AF Thunderbolt unit assigned to the 1st TAF in France. They strayed into Swiss airspace and were fired on by Swiss anti-aircraft guns, which damaged the fuel line. As a result, the pilot had to land at the next suitable place. The crew abandoned the small observation aircraft, carrying their parachutes with them, and hid in a nearby wooded area. They were picked up by some Swiss frontier guards a day later.

The Stinson L-5-WV Sentinel was dismantled and taken by train for repair. It was used by the Swiss Air Force as A-96 before being returned to Allied authorities in October of 1945.

The advance of the U.S. Army close to the Swiss border resulted in a number of violations of Swiss airspace by 9th and 15th Air Force aircraft and, in late 1944, a fighter belonging to a tactical unit was forced to land. On 15 October 1944, a P-47D-22-RE (42-26063) Thunderbolt

of the 50th FG ran into two Swiss Messerchmitt Bf 109s, which damaged the Thunderbolt, forcing it to land.

2LT Jerald Conlan intended to land in an open field with the landing gear down but recognized the field was not a suitable landing place and retracted the undercarriage. At this moment, a local anti-aircraft unit fired on the Thunderbolt, scoring hits in the engine and oil tank. Oil covered part of the windscreen and Conlan was forced the belly in the Thunderbolt in a field near Laufen. By chance, a Swiss Air Force interrogator, *Hauptmann* Von Meiss was on vacation near-by, close to the place where the Thunderbolt landed. The Swiss Captain invited the pilot home where he was allowed to have a shower, because he was competely covered in oil. Then he conducted a short interrogation over tea and cake.

On 16 November 1944, the 15th Air Force bombed the marshalling yards at Munich. After climbing over the Alps, 2LT John W. Livermore in *CHICK*, a B-24H-30-FO (42-95340) turned away from the formation and headed back towards southern Switzerland. 2LT Livermore informed his leader that he was low on fuel and could not make it back to base. For more than half an hour, the bomber circled over the Swiss-Italian border before three C-36 aircraft picked up *CHICK* and guided the Liberator to Magadino airfield.

On final approach, the ship suddenly stalled and crashed short of the runway. The accident injured three of the crew, who were taken to the nearest hospital. The entire nose section of *CHICK* was destroyed. Before the B-24H was dismantled, the Swiss found there was about 540 gallons of fuel left in the tanks.

1LT Doyle R. Smith and his crew were flying *THE LADY PATRICIA*, a B-24J-10-FO (42-51672) that was usually assigned to 1LT Daryl R. Mason, who remembered his aircraft:

We flew the ship on twenty-three missions. My crew finally decided to name it "THE LADY PATRICIA" after my one year old daughter. I was hospitalized for a few days and it was at this time that another crew took the plane out on a mission.

Prior to reaching the initial point, LT Smith lost the number three engine and fell behind and to the right of the formation. He went over the target and regaining the formation at the rally point after coming off the target. At approximately 1245, while west of Degerndorf, his number four engine went out and had to be feathered. Five minutes later he dropped out of formation and headed towards Switzerland.

The bomber circled twice over the short landing strip at Ems-Plarenga, then headed in the direction of Arosa and was seen some minutes later over Chur, circling and looking for a suitable landing field. Unable to fine a suitable field, and with the number four engine on fire, the crew bailed out and the bomber crashed close to the town of Malix. The crew was soon picked up by Swiss soldiers.

On 9 December 1944, the 15th Air Force attacked oil installations at Regensburg in Bavaria. 2LT Don R. Jacobs was leading Baker squadron in the 463rd BG in his B-17G-50-VE (44-8193) and on the way to the target his number two engine had to be feathered. To

2LT Don Jacobs landed this radar equipped Mickey ship at Altenrhein with the number two and three engines out and the props feathered. The radar on the B-17G-50-VE (44-8193) was carried in a dome that replaced the ball turret. The elevators and rudder were Yellow. (Fotohaus Wiesner)

The crew of this B-17, flown by 1LT Maurice D. Porter, bailed out over the Austrian-Swiss border and five of them were picked up by Swiss guards. The B-17G-60-DL (44-6678) crashed into mount Piz Plazer at an altitude of 9,000 feet. (Fotohaus Wiesener)

lighten the Fortress, the bombardier, 1LT Stanley J. Hagen, dropped six bombs in the Alps. Still unable to keep up with the formation, he dropped the remaining four bombs. Then the number three engine started throwing oil and at this point Don Jacobs called his deputy to take over the lead of Baker squadron. Jacobs dropped the ship out of formation and headed for Switzerland where he made a safe landing with the number two and three engines feathered.

On 25 December 1944 the 450th BG attacked the marshalling yards at Insbruck in Austria. 1LT Vincent F. Fagan was flying *MAIDEN AMERICA*, a B-24G-16-NT (42-78356) in the number two position of the first bomber box. The flak over Insbruck was moderate but accurate. *MAIDEN AMERICA* was hit in the number one engine which began to smoke. The ship dropped down about two hundred feet below the formation and, at this time, the number two engine also started to smoke. At 1140, 1LT Vincent F. Fagan headed towards Switzerland.

The pilot's initial intention was to land at Basel airport, but this area was completely covered by fog and Fagan headed for Zürich at an altitude of 12,000 feet. Over Würenlingen, the Liberator ran into heavy and accurate Swiss anti-aircraft fire which knocked out the number three engine and caused damage to the entire aircraft. The pilot gave order to bailout, and at the last second was able to change the course of *MAIDEN AMERICA*, which would have crashed into Würenlingen. As the crew bailed out they were still under Swiss fire!

Unfortunately, the copilot, 2LT Nicholas Mackoul, landed in the Aare river and drowned. 2LT Martin A. Homistek's parachute fouled on the aircraft's rudder and he was dragged down, while the tail gunner, SGT Ralph L. Coulson never jumped and perished in the wreckage. The bodies of Mackooul, Homistek and Coulson were buried at Münsingen on 28 December 1944. In September of 1965, nearly twenty-one years after the crash the local habitants of Würenlingen built a memorial for the three American airmen.

February 1945

There were no arrivals during January of 1945. On 5 February, the 15th Air Force launched an attack against oil installations in Regensburg. A B-17G-60-DL (44-6678), flown by 1LT Maurice D. Porter, lost an engine and ran short of fuel. S/SGT Kenneth L. Hoffman sent out a radio message to the Foggia station in southern Italy that they had forty gallons of fuel remaining and were trying to make it to Switzerland.

As the situation became more and more critical, LT Porter gave order to abandon ship and the crew bailed out. The aircraft was high in the Alps, and the crew was caught in a blinding snow storm, making orientation extremely difficult. The pilotless aircraft, set on autopilot headed in a southeasterly direction and crashed some thirty miles away in the Piz Plazer mountains near S-charl.

The crew became separated in the snow storm and some went the wrong way. Ball turret gunner S/SGT Christian L. Fredrickson was captured by Austrian troops two hours later on the northern slope of the *Kanzelkopf*, only a few feet from the Swiss border. The pilot Maurice Porter, copilot 2LT Donald M. Fishback and the engineer, S/SGT Charles E. Smith, were caught the following morning in the small town of Brand by a group of Wehrmacht troops. The four unfortunate Americans were sent to a prison camp at Oberursel on 10 February 1945.

In the meantime, S/SGT John P. Olinik, S/SGT Kenneth L. Hofman, S/SGT Glenn W. Machovec, S/SGT Arden O. Lannigan and S/SGT Franklin T. Wartman found shelter from the storm in a

This B-17G-100-BO (43-39018), flown by 1LT Donald D. Proctor, slid into a stone wall only 450 feet inside Switzerland. *DINAH MITE* broke its back just behind the radio operator's postion in the belly landing. (Fotohaus Wiesner)

2LT Robert F. Rhodes belly landed this P-51B-15-NA (43-24853) Mustang, named *Little Ambassador*, of the 52nd FG onto a sandbar in the Rhine River near Buchs. The five kill markings on the aircraft were scored by another pilot. (Fotohaus Wiesner)

wooden hut. They were found by Swiss frontier guards on 15 February, less than half a mile inside the border! The navigator's (F/O John E. Skoba) body was also found by the Swiss frontier guards. Upon landing he had struck a rock and crushed his skull. He was buried at Münsingen.

On 7 February 1945, North American B-25 Mitchells of the 12th Air Force attacked tactical targets in the Brenner Pass of northern Italy. LT Woodrow Sheffield was flying a B-25J-1-NA (43-4067) of the 321st Bomb Group. The ship was hit in the left wing and the pilot diverted to Switzerland. The six man crew bailed out between Bellinzona and Arbedo and the Mitchell crashed at Motto Arbino in southern Switzerland. One American was injured and was taken to a nearby the hospital.

On 22 February 1945, the 8th and 15th Air Forces launched operation CLARION, a major assault on German rail and road communications. During these raids, two 95th Bomb Group B-17s mistook the Swiss town of Stein am Rhein for Ebingen, Germany and dropped their bombs on the town causing some damage. After his return, 1LT L.A. Lenox, flying B-17G-80-BO (43-38106) coded ET-E, wrote in his interrogation form, "Area of Ebingen. Saw three buildings, roof red with big white cross. Square building about 50 x 50 feet. What are they?"

15th Air Force fighter units were also active on this day. 2LT Robert F. Rhodes was flying a P-51B-15-NA (43-24853) of the 52nd FG. Over Germany, the Mustang was hit in the oil tank, the propeller spinner and the horizontal stabilizer. Knowing that the engine would soon seize, the pilot set course for Switzerland. He belly landed the Mustang on a sand beach in the Rhine river. The belly landing severely damaged the belly of the Mustang and the engine was totally destroyed from the a lack of oil. Later a Swiss salvage team took the badly damaged Mustang to Dübendorf, where the fighter was scrapped after the war.

On 25 February 1945, the 8th Air Force sent out 1,197 heavy bombers to attack targets in Southern Germany. Five ships were reported as missing in action and three of these made it to Switzerland. It was a significant raid for Switzerland since it was the last time bombers from the "Mighty Eighth" would land here. Exactly two months later, the 8th Air Force would fly its final mission of the war.

2LT Karel Havlik and his crew were flying a B-17G-35-BO (42-31989) of the 95th Bomb Group. The ball Turret Gunner SGT George J. Hintz recalls the mission:

> *We were at 20,000 feet, approximately eight minutes from the target, when we were hit in the number four engine which began to disintegrate. Losing altitude, we turned back toward Colmar, France. We were surrounded by heavy flak and part of the nose was shot away. The wing tips were gone and the tail gunner, SGT Wilbur I. Schraner, had his guns shot out of his hands. We dropped our bombs on some town, then there was a direct hit on the number three engine and we feathered the prop.*
>
> *The oxygen bottles below the flight deck were hit and the escaping air sounded like leaking tires. The hydraulic tank above the oxygen tanks was also leaking. We prepared for a crash landing, stowing the ball turret etc, when holes appeared in the radio room walls. The radio table was hit, the number two engine caught fire and flames were blowing back over wing and the fuel cells were leaking. The word came to bailout, even though we were at low altitude. Luckily we all landed ok.*

The pilotless bomber continued on, while the crew was picked up by Swiss soldiers between Schongau and Hämikon. Swiss anti-aircraft units shot at the bomber but missed. It steadily lost altitude and after overflying the small town of Richensee, the bomber crash landed. Quite surprisingly it did not break apart, but looked as if a pilot had made a textbook belly landing.

1LT Donald D. Proctor and his crew were on a very special mission in *DINAH MITE*, a B-17G-100-BO (43-39018) "chaff ship," which was the lead ship of a group of bombers which flew ahead of the formation and dropped tinfoil to blind German radar.

Flak damaged this B-17G-35-BO (42-31989) on 1 April 1944 and the pilot made a belly landing at Honington. The Fortress was repaired and returned to the Group 19 May 1944. A short time later it would crash in Switzerland.

TOUCHY TESS, a B-17G-70-BO (43-37854), was on its 58th mission when it crash landed at Muswangen. The pilot, 2LT Charles R. Abplanalp, was killed in the crash. (Fotohaus Wiesner)

Fortress 42-31989 was flown by 2LT Karel Havlik on its last mission. The aircraft was abandoned over the Schongau - Hämikon area and the pilotless bomber glided down to a belly landing at Ermensee. It appeared as though the aircraft had made a controlled "textbook" belly landing. (Fotohaus Wiesner)

As radio operator, T/SGT Robert S. Shepherd helped load the bundles of tinfoil into the aircraft. As they worked he talked to the bombardier, 2LT Frank Bush:

Lieutenant, this is going to be a bad one today. If I do not get back, have somebody go talk to my girlfriend, OK?"

It was the only time that anyone had heard Shepherd talk that way. The bombardier, 2LT Frank Bush, recalled the mission:

We were the lead ship of a six plane element, flying between two Air Divisions. The flak over the target completely disrupted the mission. We lost two engines, had a partial loss of hydraulics and lost the radio. The radioman, Bob Shepherd, was killed by flak over Munich and the waist gunner, S/SGT Joseph Aull, and ball turret gunner, S/SGT Marbury Councell, were badly wounded.

We crossed Lake Constance and approached the Austrian/Swiss border along the Rhine river. We were not exactly certain as to our location. We came in at low level, passed over what appeared to be a pasture area near a curve in the river and a small town. We made a complete 360 turn and landed in the pasture. A big boulder caught our right wing tip and caused us to turn sharply into a dike. That was it.

Their landing place was only 400 feet inside Switzerland and soldiers from both sides came towards the ship. The Swiss were there first and took the crew into custody. The dead radio operator was buried in Münsingen. The engineer, T/SGT Louis Dobaran, told about the interrogation by a Swiss officer:

We had been told to tell everyone if we crashed that we were on a practice run. We were supposed to say all the damage was from the crash. Asked how they would explain the bullet holes in the plane, we replied practice shooting and duck hunters!

The last landing of the day was *TOUCHY TESS*, a B-17G-70-BO (43-37854) of the 351st Bomb Group, flown by 2LT Charles R. Abplanalp, a young pilot of Swiss descent. The engineer, SGT Clinton O. Norby recalled the mission:

We were all flying our second mission, except for the radio operator, SGT Paul Livingston, who had replaced the regular radioman, Stanley H. Ziegler. As we approached the time to open the bomb bay doors, Ogden called and said they were open. When I looked into the bomb bay, the doors were shut. To crank the doors open, I had to lay on my stomach with my upper body in the bomb bay, and my lower body lying on the base of the upper turret which was in the rear part of the flight deck. When they were about a third open, I heard an explosion and the bomb bay filled with black smoke. The next thing I knew, someone was shaking my feet, so I crawled back into the flight deck and there was the navigator 2LT George F. Brown standing between the pilot and copilot. The slight almost turned me sick. All across his forehead was blood which was freezing and building up over his eyes so he could not see.

Most of the damage was on the left side of the plane. The pilot's windshield, both front and side, was damaged so that he could not see out. The pilot's rudder controls were shot away, so the copilot, 2LT Harold V. Gividen, had to do the flying. By this time, we had dropped out of formation and were alone, so we asked the radio operator, SGT Paul Livingston, to call for fighter support. As it turned out, however, the radio was shot up and not working. Our number three engine stopped and our number two

LT Clayton's B-24J-15-FO (42-51974) was named *SISSY LEE*. After it arrived in Switzerland, the Swiss placed the aircraft in storage and covered the cockpit and engines with locally made covers. (Fotohaus Wiesner)

2LT Thomas P. Faulkner landed this B-24G-16-NT Liberator at Dübendorf with two damaged engines. The aircraft had a replacement rudder taken from an Olive Drab Liberator. The lower part of fin and rudder was White. (Fotohaus Wiesner)

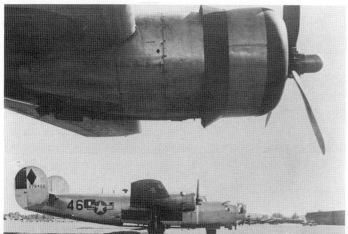

1LT Joseph C. Clayton flew this B-24J-15-FO (42-51974) to Switzerland because the number one engine was out. The cloverleaf on the rudder was the squadron marking for the 741st Bomb Squadron. The aircraft's name was carried on the starboard side. (Fotohaus Wiesner)

engine was running away, so the copilot feathered it. We had oil leaks in both the number one and number four engines.

Two of the four oxygen systems were damaged. The only oxygen systems working were for the pilot, copilot and engineer in the front of the plane, and the radio operator and the tail gunner, SGT Gene C. Bullock in the rear. In different parts of the plane, we had walk-around bottles of oxygen, so that at high altitude a crew member could leave his station and go to another part of the plane and still breath.

Because of the damage to the flight controls, the plane was not very stable, and we were gradually losing altitude. The co-pilot was working carefully so as not to lose control of the plane. The pilot's side of the plane contained the flight instruments and many of these were damaged, including both the magnetic and gyro compass. All the copilot could do was set a heading of what he could best determine was west (it turned out the be approximately southwest).

The nose area was really a mess. Part of the plexiglass was shot away and there were holes all over the left side. SGT Ernest C. Ogden had a wound in his left arm and his oxygen mask was blown off his face and his gloves were off, so he was suffering from a lack of oxygen and the cold.

After I got back to the flight deck, the pilot asked if we still had bombs in the bomb bay. I could see that the doors were still only one-third open and all bombs still there. So again, I started to crank open the doors. As I started to crank, all of a sudden the door started to open normally and I got hit on both hands by the crank.

As soon as the doors were all the way open, the pilot hit the

MAJ George L. Albin and his crew bailed out over Germany and became POWs; however, their pilotless aircraft was shot down by Swiss fighters near Trimbach. Swiss soldiers examined the wreckage for any usable items of equipment. (Peter Gunti)

salvo switch but only the bombs on the right side of the bay dropped. SGT John G. Genetti the ball turret gunner and I had to get into the bomb bay and see what was wrong. In the bomb bay, there is a lever on each shackle that can be tripped. To do this, you start with the bomb that is at the bottom or the one that goes out first. With the bomb load we had, we could not reach the lever on the bottom shackles. We were loaded with 500 pound bombs on the bottom and incendiary clusters on the top, so all we could do was start releasing the clusters first. As they dropped, they would hit the 500 pounders, break apart and fall out of the bay. We could only hope that none of them would start to burn. While Genetti and I were doing this, one of us would hold on to the other so we would not to fall out.

During all this time, the pilot, copilot and navigator were frantically working trying to determine where we were. At this time, someone called on the intercom that there were four enemy fighters at 3 o'clock high and I saw another four at 9 o'clock high. When the fighters came closer and still did not fire on us, I wondered why they had a red square with a white cross painted on the fuselage. We assumed we were over Switzerland, but we were not sure.

By now, I could see that we were going to crash, and not on a flat piece of ground. I stood up behind the pilot's seat and braced my head against the armor plate which is at the back of the seat. Just before I put my head behind the armor plating, I looked at the air speed and it was indicating 140 mph. This surprised me as we usually cruised at 130 mph indicating. Three things came to my mind: this was going to be a bad crash, we still had over 1,000 gallons of gas onboard and I was worried about fire.

I was looking out the window behind the copilot and was very amazed to see the tops of trees going over the top of the wing. It reminded me of a knife cutting them down. Also, for the first time, I was aware of no noise from the engines. I do not know when they quite running. The only noise was from the plane hitting the trees. It seemed like a long time before we came to a stop. When we finally stopped, there was a very violent motion, a centrifugal force of being thrown to your right. The last tree we hit was a very large one and we hit on the left side of the plane, wrapped around it and stopped. There is one thing that I will always remember and that is just before we hit the last tree the pilot yelled "Don't," and I often wondered what he was referring to.

When we finally stopped, I saw smoke off to my left. Again there was the fear of fire. My left foot was trapped in the wreckage. As I looked forward between the pilot and copilot, there was a mass of wreckage pushed forward so that I could not see either of them.

I could see someone's arm hanging down from between the two seats and quite a lot of blood running down from between the two seats. The copilot told me that the pilot was hurt and looked bad. The top of the plane from just below the windshield back to the top turret dome was sheared off. This in itself should have got the pilot, copilot and me — it did kill the pilot.

CAPT Leonard Smith landed this overall Blue-Gray Pathfinder B-17G-50-VE (44-8187) with two engines out and feathered and very little fuel remaining in the tanks. The aircraft was a squadron lead ship in the 99th Bomb Group. (Karl Hänggi)

The copilot, navigator, gunner Ogden and waist gunner Berlin were immediately taken from the crash site to the hospital at Lucerne. Charles Abplanalp was buried at Münsingen on 1 March 1945.

On 27 February 1945, the 15th Air Force bombed the marshalling yards at Augsburg near Munich. For the last time during the Second World War, a large number of American aircraft had to seek refuge in Switzerland.

In addition to the heavies of the 15th Air force, a B-25J-1-NA (43-4076) of the 321st BG, 12th Air Force also crashed in Switzerland. The Mitchell was piloted by 1LT Milford A. Smith. This formation was briefed to bomb targets in the Brenner Pass area. The ship reached Switzerland by flying over the Bernina Pass and as the bomber circled over Samedan, the right engine began to smoke. At that point, the crew left the burning plane. One of the crew members broke his leg when he landed and was taken into the hospital. The Mitchell crashed at Celerina, close to the bobsled run at St. Moritz.

1LT Ray M. Grooms flew a B-24J-20-FO (44-48775) to Augsburg. In addition to the regular crew, SGT Wynfield S. Clayton was aboard as an aerial photographer. Just before the target the Liberator had the number one and three engines shot out by flak. The plane continued on to the target, dropped the bomb load, then turned off the target and headed toward Switzerland.

Flak had damaged the control cables for the number three and four engines, and they could not be controlled by the pilot. All the oil was gone on engine number one and only the number two engine worked properly. Luckily they were able to make a safe landing at Altenrhein.

The B-24J was repaired by Swiss ground crew and the defective engines were replaced. On 26 March 1945, the ship took off again with Oberst Högger and Wachtmeister Schraner at the controls. Unfortunately not all anti-aircraft units along the ferry route were notified and in the area of Effretikon, flak units fired on the ship. The large Swiss markings and Red-White identification stripes on the wings and fuselage had not prevented the Liberator from being a victim of friendly fire and a few rounds hit the aircraft just behind the pilot's seat.

1LT Thomas P. Faulkner's B-24G-16-NT (42-78458) was hit over the target and at 1359, Faulkner attempted to call the lead ship but received no answer. His call was acknowledged by 1LT Loren S. Loomis who took this message, "I am losing five hundred feet per minute and I am going to a neutral country." The Liberator dropped out of formation and was escorted by a number of P-38s towards the Swiss border. The flak had knocked out the number two and three engines, the latter being completely locked. Shortly after crossing the border, Swiss Morane fighters intercepted and guided the stricken bomber to Dübendorf, where it landed normally.

1LT Donald K. Fotheringham and crew flew a brand new B-24 L-15-FO (44-49928) to Augsburg. Along for the ride was PVT Herbert C. Vochatzer, who was assigned to the regular crew as an aerial photographer. The ship was hit by flak just before bombs away and the bomb load was immediately dropped. Once the bombs were away, LT Fotheringham headed for Switzerland. With very little fuel left, the Liberator landed with its Swiss fighter escort at Dübendorf.

The new aircraft was studied by a number of Swiss engineers and specialists. On 10 and 11 April Oberst Högger and Wachtmeister Schraner carried out evaluation flights. Then on 3 and 5 May, supercharger tests were made, and on these occasions three engine specialists, Messrs. Keller, Boller and Carraux flew as observers.

1LT Joseph C. Clayton was flying SISSY LEE, a B-24J-15-FO (42-51974) that carried five, instead of the usual four, gunners. Just before the target, 1LT Clayton dropped out of the formation with the number one engine smoking badly. He reported over the radio that he would try to make it to Switzerland since he had engine trouble. He was escorted to Dübendorf, where he made a safe landing.

1LT Douglas W. Lambert and his crew flew a B-24J-15-FO (42-51903) that was seriously damaged by a burst of flak which exploded directly under the starboard wing. LT Lambert had to feather the number four engine and the number two engine began to smoke. At 1425 they left the formation near Füssen and headed for Switzerland.

The ship was picked up by Swiss fighters but because of the damage they unable to follow them to Dübendorf and the crew

1LT Donald K. Fotheringham landed this B-24L-15-FO (44-49928) at Dübendorf with only twenty-four gallons of fuel remaining on board. The small bulged window under the larger navigator's window was a field modification. (Swiss Air Force)

bailed out over the town of Dietikon and two of them were slightly injured as they hit the ground. The pilotless Liberator headed toward central Switzerland and fighters were scrambled to intercept the aircraft. Near Lucerne, the Moranes opened fire and some minutes later flames came out of the engine and fuselage. Finally, the bomber crashed into a wooded area between Meggen and Adligenswil.

CAPT Leonard Smith and his crew were flying a radar-equipped B-17G-50-VE (44-8187) of the 99th BG. The regular copilot, LT Conrad Headley, had been replaced by 1LT John B. Morat and they had a new bombardier, 2LT Walter A. Mucek. Leonard Smith recalled:

We were not flying our assigned ship "Bugs Buddy Budda Doc" on this particular mission, instead we were flying a "Mickey" radar plane. Our crew was flying the lead ship of the last Squadron in the 99th Bomb Group, referred to as "Tail End Charlie" and we were the last Group to fly over the target at Augsburg. We came in low for a bomb drop — 22,500 feet. Most of my missions were flown at 26,000 feet and above. The flak was deadly accurate and inflicted severe damage to our plane and others in our squadron.

The tail gunner S/SGT Victor A. Fabiniak added:

The flak over the target was so heavy that you could probably walk on it. Coming off the target, we had to abort the formation, and the pilot called on the intercom to throw everything out of the plane and disarm our weapons. We were losing altitude and were preparing to bailout if we had to. I then came up to the waist position from the tail, looked out of the window and there they were two Swiss fighters. They escorted us to Dübendorf airfield.

2LT Ralph V. Elliott was flying a brand new B-24L-5-FO (44-49421) and on the return from Augsburg, while over the Alps, he discovered that they had only 200 gallons of fuel. This would not allow them to reach their home base at Giulia and at 1507, he dropped out of formation and headed towards Switzerland. When the Liberator touched down at Dübendorf there was very little fuel remaining in the tanks.

An experienced crew with high ranking officers was leading the 97th Bomb Group in a Mickey (radar equipped) B-17G-55-VE (44-8248). The crew included the pilot, MAJ George L. Albin, the copilot MAJ John B. Campbell, the navigator, CAPT Billy F. Bolton, radar operator 1LT Alvin F. Smith, bombardier 1LT Robert M. Martin and five enlisted men.

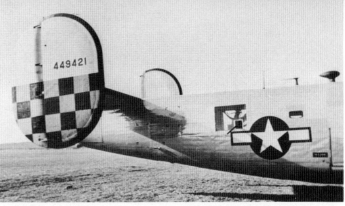

2LT Ralph V. Elliott diverted to Switzerland with his B-24L-5-FO (44-49421) Liberator due to a fuel shortage, when he landed there was only 190 gallons left in the tanks. The Yellow-Black checkerboard on the lower fin and rudder were the markings of the 459th Bomb Group. (Fotohaus Wiesner)

The Fortress was hit by accurate flak over the target and was seen by other 97th BG ships loosing altitude and heading in a northesterly direction. Some ten minutes later, about 1325, the aircraft commander gave order to bailout. MAJ Albin set the stricken ship on autopilot and the crew left the Fortress in two groups.

The copilot, navigator, radio operator S/SGT Harold C. Isaacson and tail gunner S/SGT Richard L. Adkins were taken in custody by local German policemen at Füssen, while the rest of the crew was captured by the Wehrmacht near Kaufbeuren. They all spent the rest of the war in various POW camps.

The Fortress continued to fly its plotted course and a little over an hour later, the B-17 entered Swiss airspace. The ghost-bomber was soon intercepted by Swiss fighters, which tried to guide it to Dübendorf airfield. All the signs given by the Swiss to surrender and follow them were not acknowledged and the bomber continued on its preprogramed course. Finally, the leader of the Morane flight gave order to shoot down the Flying Fortress near the city of Olten and the fighters opened fire. A fire broke out on the right wing and the bomber began loosing altitude as it approached the town of Trimbach. A Swiss fighter continued to pursue it, firing all the way. Shortly after the bomber passed Trimbach it crashed and was completely destroyed.

The local police and military personnel were quite surprised when they found no trace of the crew.

1LT Ray M. Grooms succeeded in landing his badly damaged B-24J-20-FO (44-48775) Liberator at Altenrhein. The propeller on the number four engine was feathered and the number one and three engines were damaged. (Karl Hänggi)

March 1945

On 24 March 1945, the 15th Air Force again bombed targets in the Munich area, as well the final assembly plant for Messerschmitt Me 262s at Neuburg/Donau. The 459th BG was briefed to bomb the Munich-Riem airfield and among this force was 2LT Conrad C. Alder, flying a B-24J-195-CO (44-41075) Liberator. On this mission the crew had no navigator assigned. The copilot F/O Robert A. Long told about the mission:

We sustained flak damaged over the target. The number three engine lost oil pressure and the cylinder head temperature was rising. When the number three feathering button was pressed — nothing happened. The drag of the windmilling number three prevented a trip over the Alps. Our code call of the day was transmitted, "Sungold A for Able - Firtree - calling Little Joe," which meant a 459th Group A Box aircraft was in trouble, heading toward Switzerland and were there any fighters available for cover? We crossed Lake Constance and were joined by three Morane fighters. We fired red flares and lowered the landing gear. They guided us to Dübendorof where we landed. At Dübendorf, a quick look at the number three engine revealed a triangular hole in the number three reduction gear housing.

This B-24J-195-CO (44-41075) Liberator, flown by 2LT Conrad C. Alder, had a damaged number three engine. The sharkmouth was the unit marking of the 756th Bomb Squadron. (Fotohaus Wiesner)

The navigator 1LT Clifford R. Bilek recalled:

Our approach to the target was lower than briefed, why, I will never know. The mountains at the north end of the Brenner Pass are about 8,000 feet and we were at about 18,000 feet — German 88s are deadly at this altitude. We were flying in the number two position and the first burst of flak blew the number one aircraft apart and he went down in flames. We automatically took over the bomb run but not for long, as the second salvo, I believe four shells, caught us and exploded under the number two engine and all along the length of the aircraft from the nose to the tail. The plane pitched down and to the right and the pilots had quite a time getting it under control again. The Liberator was a mess and the decision was made to try to get to France rather than back to our base which was further away. As we crossed Switzerland, we tossed out every thing that was possible to lighten the aircraft, since that old beast was having a hard time staying in the air. Swiss fighters intercepted us and signaled for us to land, which we did. During the landing I tied the two parachutes to the waist windows and one of the gunners and I deployed them after touchdown which helped us considerably to slow the aircraft. The ground was a most welcome sight that day.

8 April 1945

On 8 April 1945, the 15th Air Force raided important strongpoints near the Brenner Pass. This were the last Liberators to seek refuge in Switzerland during the war.

STRANGE CARGO, a B-24J-10-FO (42-51623), was flown by 2LT Richard Turk. The ship had been damaged by flak which knocked out the number one engine. Additionally, the radio operator, SGT Frank Kovacs, was wounded in the leg from shell fragments. As a reuslt, the crew made the decision to seek refuge in Switzerland. About seven miles south of Lake Constance, the STRANGE CARGO entered Swiss airspace. A safe landing was made at Dübendorf and Frank Kovacs was quickly taken to the hospital.

The 98th Bomb Group was briefed to bomb the Vipiteno railroad bridge in northern Italy. 1LT Robert E. McKee and his crew were assigned to fly a B-24J-2-NT (42-78600) which carried two names, DOPEY (a Walt Disney cartoon character) was painted left side of the nose and a pretty girl, KATHRYN ANNE, was carried on the right side. In addition to the regular crew, 1LT Arthur G. Smallwood, a professional cameraman from Hollywood, California was assigned to the crew. His duty was to take combat movies for the Army Air Force.

STRANGE CARGO carried the Yellow and Black tail markings of the 450th Bomb Group. The B-24J-10-FO (42-51623) had numerous patches on the fin where ground crews had repaired previous flak damage. (Fotohaus Wiesner)

2LT Richard Turk diverted to Switzerland with his B-24J-10FO (42-51623) Liberator named STRANGE CARGO. The blister window on the nose was a field modification. (Fotohaus Wiesner)

16 April 1945

On 16 April 1945, the 387th Bomb Group, based at Clastres, France dispatched thirty-eight B-26 Marauders to attack targets around Kempten. 1LT Raymond W. Reid flew as deputy lead in a B-26G-15-MA (44-67894) of the 559th Squadron. The engineer SGT Robert L. Mercado recalled:

> On 16 April 1945, I was flying my 29th mission. We were on a mission into southern Germany and near our target, we were hit by a flak shell which did not explode but did hit the right engine of our B-26, ripping the engine apart and tearing a large hole in the copilot's side of the airplane. The concussion knocked the copilot from his seat and dazed him. The pilot called me in the upper turret and told me that we'd been hit and to come down and help him, which I did. At the same time the pilot gave the alarm to abandon the plane, at which time the tail and waist gunners, SGTS Johnnie F. Jones and Earl L. Theis, bailed out over the Black Forest. One was captured by the Germans and the other swam across the Rhine river into Switzerland.
>
> The copilot, 2LT Kenneth J. Stear and myself persuaded the pilot to stay with the airplane until we reached the Rhine river, knowing this was the border between Germany and Switzerland. When we sighted the Rhine river and since our plane was losing altitude rapidly, we bailed out. The copilot landed just inside Switzerland, the pilot's parachute did not open and he was killed. We landed near the town of Rheinfelden, where the Swiss Army captured us. The plane hit a mountain and blew up.

McKee's Liberator carried a painting of _DOPEY_ on the port side of the nose and a second name, _Kathryn Anne_, on the starboard side. _DOPEY_ was a character from Walt Disney's "Snow White and the Seven Dwarfs." (Fotohaus Wiesner)

1LT Robert McKee's B-24J-2-NT (42-78600) was the last Liberator to seek refuge in Switzerland. The crew diverted when a flak shell knocked out the number three engine. There were some 300 holes found in the aircraft. (Fotohaus Wiesner)

Swiss soldiers cleaned up the crash site at Zuzgen and 1LT Reid was buried at Münsingen, he was the last American airman killed over Switzerland.

The Last Arrival 20 April 1945

Ironically the last American aircraft to land in Switzerland, arrived on Adolf Hitler's birthday, 20 April. The 15th Air Force once again bombed strongpoints along the strategic Brenner Pass. The 301st BG was briefed to bomb the Vipiteno marshalling yards in northern Italy. 1LT Robert M. Adams and his crew flew _PRINCESS O'ROURKE_, a B-17G-50-DL (44-6347) of the 301st Bomb Group. They flew as ship number 31 in the low, left squadron, a corner which was usually exposed to flak.

Flak over the target damaged the Flying Fortress and the ship fell back behind the formation. At this time, 1LT Adams notified the command pilot that he was going to attempt to land in Switzerland or France. The flak damaged the oil tanks on both the number one and number four engines, and both were had to be feathered. As a result it was impossible to stay with the formation. At 1228, near the Austrian-Italian border, the bomber left the formation. On the way to Switzerland the crew jettisoned both tail guns and the ball turret.

Swiss fighters intercepted the Flying Fortress and 1LT Adams followed them to Dübendorf airfield where they made a safe landing on the two inboard engines. Three weeks later, the Germans surrendered and the war in Europe was over.

PRINCESS O'ROURKE, a B-17G-50-DO (44-6347) landed with the number one and number four engines shut down and feathered. 1LT Robert Adams and his crew were the last American airmen to seek refuge in Switzerland. The Flying Fortress was jacked up for a landing gear drop check before is was flown to Burtonwood, England on 1 September 1945. (Fotohaus Wiesner)

Swiss Flights

With the arrival of American aircraft in Switzerland, the Swiss Air Force became very interested in obtaining technical information about these aircraft. At the beginning, there was some doubt about the legality of using interned aircraft, since these aircraft were still the property of the USAAF.

The Swiss Air Force was interested in obtaining data about the range and angle of fire of the .50 caliber machine guns aboard the bombers with the aim of developing the best tactics for attacking the aircraft. This was necessary in case a foreign bomber would not willingly follow the Swiss fighters to a landing site. The Swiss had a healthy respect for the strong defensive fire of the .50 caliber machine guns installed in the B-17 and B-24.

Additionally, the Swiss Air Force and Swiss Aviation Industry were very interested in obtaining information on the performance of these new American bombers. Such large four engined aircraft were rather unknown in Switzerland and there was very little information available about the construction and other "secrets" of these bombers. The Swiss aviation industry expected to gain some "know-how" from the American designs, which they hoped to adapt to their own designs.

B-17s and B-24s were tested at the Test and Experimental Center at Emmen. Of particular interest were the turbosuperchargers and engines. Engines and other equipment from the bombers were given to private factories and universities for further investigation. Other items, such as fuel and parachutes were closely examined and the results of these tests were closely compared with the similar products from the Swiss National Aviation Industry.

All newly arrived American bombers were checked to see if there was any new equipment on it which was unknown to the Swiss. All new improvements, such as the chin or "Cheyenne" turrets on the Boeing B-17G were tested and investigated. The Swiss Interrogation Officers always asked crews about newly introduced equipment or new combat tactics. The Swiss soon had a good working knowledge of the hardware used by the Americans, as well as their combat tactics and order of battle, mainly by gathering bits and pieces of information.

This B-17G-35-BO (42-32073) was used to develop suitable combat tactics against the Flying Fortress. Its first flight in Swiss markings took place on 1 June 1944, with Oberst Högger and Oberleutnant Heitmaneck at the controls. Two American pilots were aboard to act as instructors. (Fotohaus Wiesner)

The same procedures were also followed with British, Italian and German aircraft and crews who came to Switzerland. The problem with the four engined American aircraft was their size. Swiss pilots had no prior experience with such large aircraft. The largest aircraft the Swiss had experience with was the Swissair Douglas DC-2s and DC-3s and the three engined Junkers Ju-52. Even at the end of the war, only a few Swiss pilots had been instructed and authorized to fly the heavy four engined bombers.

Of the first four intact American aircraft that landed in Switzerland, the Swiss chose a B-17F-105-BO (42-30478) the latest variant of the Flying Fortress available, as a test bed. At this time the chief in charge of the Technical Department of the Swiss Air Force at Dübendorf, Oberst (Colonel) Karl Högger, flew all interned foreign aircraft. These were mostly single and twin engined aircraft of German design. These did not cause him too much trouble, but the B-17F would require some special precautions.

Högger's technical assistant was Wachtmeister (T/SGT) Franz Schraner. Högger, Schraner and Oberleutant (1LT) Borner began by studying the B-17s cockpit. Franz Schraner recalled:

> At the beginning, we really had no idea on the characteristics of the Flying Fortress. Personally I was very impressed with the size and the workmanship of these gigantic four engined aircraft. We sat in the cockpit of the Flying Fortress and began to investigate every switch and light. Fortunately, we had some slight knowledge of English. Once we established an idea of the workings of the bomber's cockpit, we began to establish a check list.
>
> We tested the rudder control mechanism and then we started the engines. As a further step we jacked up the aircraft and drop tested the undercarriage. We went over our check list over and over again, until we had some training and felt familiar with the controls of the Fortress.

Oberst Högger and Oberleutnant Borner take off in B-17F-95-BO (42-30233) on 3 May 1944 from Altenrhein airfield. The runway was short and had a grass surface, making takeoffs with four engined bombers very difficult. (Franz Schraner)

Wachtmeister Franz Schraner at the controls of a B-24 Liberator. Together with Oberst Karl Högger, he was responsible for ferrying most of the American aircraft to Dübendorf airfield. (Franz Schraner)

This B-17G-30-DL (42-38204) was flown by Oberst Högger and Wacht-meister Schraner from Geneva-Cointrin to Dübendorf on 13 July 1945. No guns were carried and, although Swiss markings have been added, the original Group and Squadron markings were still on the bomber. (Franz Schraner)

Oberst Högger and Wachtmeister Schraner flew this B-17G-50-VE (44-8193) from Altenrhein to Dübendorf on 23 December 1944, with mechanics Wehrli and Denzler on board as passengers. High visibility markings were carried to hopefully prevent friendly AA units from firing on the aircraft. (Fotohaus Wiesner)

The next step was to conduct taxi tests at Dübendorf and after we felt that we had enough experience, we took off for the first experimental flight. Nothing unusual happened and we safely returned to Dübendorf. On one of the early flights; however, we filled the wrong tanks with fuel and shortly after take off, both inboard engines quit. We were able to handle the problem and came down safely.

All the flights were made with full Swiss markings and due to the short runway, the maximum gross weight was limited to about 20 tons. All Swiss pilots involved in the flight tests praised the flight characteristics of the B-17F and found the aircraft quite easy to fly. The only problem were the four engines and the size of the aircraft.

After at least four training and familiarization flights, the B-17F-120-BO *IMPATIENT VIRGIN II* was ferried to Emmen for other research programs. With the permission of the American Embassy, 1LT Martin Andrews, who landed his B-17F-25-VE (42-5841) at Magadino on 6 September 1943, was sent to Dübendorf to assist the Swiss with flight testing the B-17F.

On 22 October 1943, the Swiss ferried a bomber from one location to another for the first time. Such an undertaking needed some preparations: all anti-aircraft units along the route had to be notified of the date and time of the ferry flight. In addition, large Swiss markings were painted on the aircraft and most of the flights were made at 3,000 feet or below.

Oberst Högger acted as pilot, Oberleutnant Borner as copilot and Wachtmeister Schraner as engineer were joined by Mechanic Johner to ferry the B-17F-25-VE (42-5841) from Magadino to the Test and Research Center at Emmen. At 1449, the bomber took off from Magadino. Wachtmeister Schraner recalls:

Anything not necessary to fly the aircraft had been removed from the ship. In addition, we had only enough fuel on board to make the flight over the Alps. Everything worked well, but during the flight, Oberleutnant Borner engaged the autopilot and we immediately lost control of the aircraft. Luckily for us we managed to turn off the autopilot, but Oberst Högger told Borner to never do this again.

The first intact B-24 arrived in Switzerland during January of 1944 but due to the bad winter weather testing was limited to static research. Flight testing from the snow covered, soft, wet ground was considered too dangerous.

On 25 April 1944, two undamaged B-24 Liberators landed at Dübendorf and both aircraft were test flown in Swiss markings. Robert Lehman, a professional pilot who flew four engined passenger aircraft before he was assigned to the 448th Bomb Group, remained as instructor at Dübendorf. He assisted CAPT Robert L. Cardenas to train Swiss pilots on the Liberator. The first flight took place on 28 April 1944, when Oberst Högger and Wachtmeister Schraner took one of the Liberators (serial 42-64496) on a test flight.

The Liberator (42-64496) was also used for a propaganda film to show the Swiss how foreign intruders were intercepted and forced to land. In the film, the Liberator carried no national markings. The film was intended as a morale booster, since foreign (mostly Allied) bomber formations frequently flew over Switzerland and most of them could not be intercepted. This was because the formations stayed over Swiss airspace for only a short time.

Swiss crews perform an engine change on this B-17F-25-VE (42-5841) at Emmen during the Summer of 1945. A number of trials were conducted at Emmen during the war before Oberst Högger and Wachtmeister Schraner flew the bomber from Emmen to Dübendorf on 5 Septmber 1945. Here the bomber was turned over to the USAFF. (Franz Schraner)

Swiss markings were applied to this B-24H-20-DT (41-28948) while the ship was hangared at Basel-Birsfelden. Carrying full Swiss markings, the ship took part in an air show at Basel-Birsfelden on 13 September 1945. Before it was turned back to the USAAF, the aircraft was repainted with American markings. (Franz Schraner)

Between 3 and 8 July 1944, a special instruction course for pilots of the Überwachungsgeschwader (Surveillance Unit) was held. These men were professional military pilots and had participated in many escort missions guiding American bombers to Swiss bases. Most of the pilots, however, lacked practical experience on how to attack these large aircraft; they had only a theoretical knowledge of the best angles of attack and the weak points on an American bomber.

During this training period, mock attacks were flown against B-17s and B-24s flown by Swiss pilots. During these trials, pilots of the Überwachungsgeschwader were also given the opportunity to ride in a B-17 as a passengers. On 6 July 1944, Oberst Högger carried thirteen pilots in ship 42-32073 and another twelve pilots were flown the following day. Oberleutnat Rageth, the Commander of the Surveillance Unit, acted as copilot on some of the trials evaluating his pilots as they made attack runs in their Morane fighters.

Swiss fighters pilots were briefed to guide the American bombers to either Dübendorf or Payerne airfields, in order to concentrate the bomber fleet in these two places but, in some cases, a bomber landed on another airfield. Ferrying these aircraft to Dübendorf or Payerne became an almost routine job for Oberst Högger and Wachtmeister Schraner from mid-1944 to the end of the war.

Wachtmeister Schraner recalled:

> Takeoffs from short fields like Magadino and Altenrhein were quite difficult. Especially Altenrhein, which had a wavy grass runway which ended in Lake Constance. As a result we always took off with full power on all engines in direction of Lake Constance; at the end was a fence we had to climb over and then dive a little bit in order to gain more speed. We then turned over the lake and headed for Dübendorf. That was it!
>
> Usually these ferry flights were uneventful, but some were not. Once we ferried a Liberator from Geneva-Cointrin to Payerne, and the airspeed indicator failed during the flight. Only the duplicate instrument in the navigator's compartment was still working. So I moved there and wrote our speed on small slips I showed Colonel Högger through the astrodome; it worked perfectly and it was one of the softest landings we ever made.
>
> Even though all the anti-aircraft units along the route were notified about our ferry flight and we carried Swiss markings, there was always a danger of being shot at by friendly anti-aircraft units. It happened the first time when we flew a B-17 from Magadino to Dübendorf. Near Biasca, we were shot at by our own guns. We continued to fly to Dübendorf and after we landed COL Högger went to the phone and talked with the commander of the AA Unit. I think Högger had some harsh word for him.

Even the high visibility neutrality markings did not prevent this B-24J-20-FO (44-48775) from being damaged by friendly anti-aircraft fire on the ferry flight from Altenrhein to Dübendorf on 26 March 1945. Fragments hit behind the pilot's seat, but fortunately, no one was injured. (Daniel Keller via Martin Kyburz)

> On another occasion, we were on a flight with a B-24 from Altenrhein, and as we prepared for the landings at Dübendorf we were fired on. They scored hits on a propeller, in one of the spinners and on the flight deck behind the crew. Finally we made a safe landing, shaken, but happy that we were still alive.

GEN Legge, the U.S. Military Attache in Switzerland, had a growing interest in aviation. The General had came to Switzerland before the war, not knowing he would spend the here. As a former cavalry officer, he had more knowledge of horse riding than in horsepower. He was quite interested in visiting Dübendorf to inspect the aircraft and the equipment the American airmen were carrying.

The Swiss invited him to Dübendorf and showed him all of the equipment including both bomber types and explaining each aircraft in detail. A flight in both a B-17 and a B-24 was on the program during the General's visit to Dübendorf on 8 August 1944. At 1034, Oberst Högger and Wachtmeister Schraner took off in a B-17G-35-BO (42-32073) with GEN Legge, Swiss COL Wuhrmann and CAPT G. von Meiss aboard. The flight lasted some thirty minutes. Afterward, the guests boarded a B-24G-17-NT (42-78439) which had arrived five days earlier due to a failed oxygen system. In addition to Legge, Wuhrmann and von Meiss, 2LT Sergres from the U.S. Embassy also took part in the flight.

Franz Schraner recalled:

> General Legge was quite interested in these aircraft and we always had a hard time preventing his touching the switches and buttons in the cockpit. Suddenly, we heard a noise and then a strong draft in the flight deck, followed by a lot of dust whirling around. We discovered that General Legge somehow had pushed the button releasing the emergency escape hatch on top of the cockpit. The hatch fell into the flight deck and caused the strong draft.
>
> As we proceeded to land, we discovered that the nosewheel would not lower and, while COL Högger circled, I cranked down the nosewheel manually. We made it back to Dübendorf safely.

BORSUK'S BITCH had its 453rd BG markings overpainted and the American insignia replaced by Swiss crosses. Oberst Hogger and Wachtmeister Schraner flew this B-24H-10-CF (42-64496) for the first time on 28 April 1944. (H.J. Dubler)

This Stinson L-5-WV (42-99186) was repaired by Swiss ground crews and repainted in full Swiss neutrality markings and the Swiss code A-96. The aircraft was later sold to the Alpar AG Company and given the civil registration HB-TRY. (Karl Hänggi)

After the war, the L-5 was purchased by Alpar AG and given the civil registration HB-TRY. The aircraft was based at Berne-Belp airfield. (Swiss Air Force Museum)

One aircraft which was probably of higher interest to the Swiss than the bomber types was the North American P-51 Mustang. Even before its arrival in Switzerland, the Swiss knew it was an excellent fighter. On 19 July 1944, 1LT Curtis Simpson landed his P-51B at Ems-Plarenga. Oberst Högger initially wanted to fly the aircraft out from the short strip, but the lack of available data on the aircraft led his commander to order it shipped by rail to Dübendorf. With the U.S. markings replaced by Swiss crosses, the Mustang flew again on 1 August 1944 and several test flights were made by various experienced Swiss pilots. They all considered the Mustang as a super fighter in its performance and flying characteristics.

Eventually, the fighter was flown to the Test and Research center at Emmen where further tests were carried out. The positive experience the Swiss Air Force had with the Mustang led to the purchase of 130 ex-USAAF P-51Ds after the war. The Mustang became the last piston engined fighter purchased by the Swiss Air Force, being replaced by British De Havilland Vampire jets.

The Stinson L-5-WV (42-99186) also saw use as a liaison aircraft in the Swiss Air Force. It served with Swiss Air Force markings as A-96. In October of 1945, the L-5 was returned to the USAAF. The L-5, however, never left Swiss soil since it was purchased by the Swiss company Alpar AG. This company registered the aircraft HB-TRY and during 1966, the *Segelfluggruppe Thun* (Glider Sport Association) at Thun took over the L-5 and used the plane as a glider tug. Two years later, the L-5 was struck from the civil register and it is in storage, awaiting restoration. The Stinson is the only interned American aircraft that remained more or less intact in Switzerland.

This P-51B-10-NA (42-106438) was repaired and test flown at Dübendorf on 1 August 1944. At this time, only the upper portion of the rudder was painted Red and the D-Day invasion stripes were still on the Mustang. (Fotohaus Wiesner)

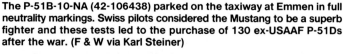

The P-51B-10-NA (42-106438) underwent a number of tests and trials at Emmen. The Mustang was repainted in the neutrality paint scheme ordered on 16 September 1944. The rudder was Red, while engine cowling was White. The fuselage and wings carried Red/White bands as well as large Swiss national insignia. (F & W Emmen via Karl Steiner)

The P-51B-10-NA (42-106438) parked on the taxiway at Emmen in full neutrality markings. Swiss pilots considered the Mustang to be a superb fighter and these tests led to the purchase of 130 ex-USAAF P-51Ds after the war. (F & W via Karl Steiner)

B-17s and B-24s line the grass area of Dübendorf during the Summer of 1945. Many of these aircraft were overhauled and flown out to the USAAF depot at Burtonwood, England. (Fotohaus Wiesner)

Swiss ground crews conduct an overhaul of the inboard engine of *FRECKLES*, a B-17G-35-DL (42-107092). The Flying Fortress was flown out to Burtonwood, England on 1 September 1945. (Weltwoche Bilderarchiv)

Return Flights

During the Second World War, a total of 166 American aircraft came to Switzerland, forty-one were totally destroyed in crashes, thirty-nine were badly damaged, but another eighty-six were considered as repairable. As more American aircraft sought refuge in Switzerland and space at Dübendorf became scarce, the Swiss began to dismantle the more heavily damaged aircraft for storage in hangars at Dübendorf and Kloten.

The interned aircraft were maintained during the war by a force of about thirty to forty Swiss Air Force maintenance men. The tires were placed on boards and chocked, front and rear. The propellers were pulled through once a week and the engines were preflighted at varying intervals.

On 7 November 1944, a Technical Commission from the 8th Air Force Service Command arrived at Dübendorf to inspect the aircraft. The five men were under the command of LTCOL Peter DePaolo. The commission found the interned aircraft in a very good condition, considering the length of time they had been inactive. Some Liberators were found to have wet flight decks, due to rain water seeping in around the top turret.

The commission helped the Swiss Air Force with advice and information on maintenance requirements of the American bombers. Prior to their arrival, approximately ten per cent of the aircraft were covered with protective canvas covers manufactured by the Swiss Air Force; however, a shortage of material forced this work to be discontinued. As a result, canvas was delivered by the USAAF to allow all the aircraft which were unsheltered to be covered (with the exception of the L-5, the P-51B, a B-17G at Geneva and a B-24 at Basel-Birsfelden).

An American ground crewman begins to cut up one of the B-17 Flying Fortress bombers that were scrapped at Dübendorf. The B-17G-30-BO (42-31889) had been flown by the 2nd BG before coming to Switzerland. (A. Kistler)

This B-24H-1-FO (42-7519) is up on jacks for a landing gear drop check. The Liberator landed at Dübendorf on 7 January 1944 and was flown out to Burtonwood on 8 October 1945. (Franz Schraner)

B-17G (42-31889) has been cut in half just to the rear of the radio compartment bulkhead. All four engines as well as all weapons have already been removed. (A. Kistler)

The thirty-eight dismantled aircraft stored at Dübendorf and Kloten were classified as scrap by the commission, since they had been dismantled by inexperienced personnel and there was a lack of the proper equipment for re-assembly. Some 152 engines were stored at Kloten and Zürich and parts from these along with other salvaged parts were later used to repair aircraft selected to be flown out of Switzerland.

On 8 May 1945 the war in Europe ended, but the Swiss Government did not allow any aircraft to be repaired or flown out to England until the war with Japan ended on 15 September. Three days later, the first C-87s and C-47s arrived in Switzerland with ground crews and equipment. During the landing of the first C-87 at Dübendorf, the pilots made a costly mistake and the transport crashed into a wooded area near Dübendorf and four airmen were killed. During the following weeks, 290 transports landed at Dübendorf, bringing tools, spare parts, ferry crews and other essential items. These aircraft also transported surplus engines and other interned equipment (including bombs) to München-Erding.

The American mechanics, assisted by Swiss mechanics, began to overhaul the bombers. The engines were checked, as well the electrical systems, brakes and landing gear. If necessary, the engines were changed and other repairs were made.

Acceptance flights were made on all the B-17s but were conducted on only a portion of the B-24s. On 27 August 1945, the first three B-17s were flown out of Dübendorf. These aircraft carried only minimum fuel, enough to reach either München-Erding or Paris-Villacoublay, where the aircraft were refueled for the trip to Burtonwood, the large USAAF depot in England. A takeoff with a full fuel load was felt to be too dangerous since the runway at Dübendorf was considered too short.

Every week about seven to eight bombers were flown out and all were ferried without armament. On 27 August, shortly after take off, one of the three departing B-17s had the plexiglas dome of the top turret blow off and fall onto a street in Dübendorf. Luckily no one was injured. On the way to Munich-Erding, the crew of the B-24H-15-FO (42-52347) *BELLE RINGER* ran into bad weather. They headed toward Paris-Villacoublay but got lost and ran out of fuel. The aircraft was completely destroyed in the crash landing. Fortunately, none of the crew were injured.

The front half of the fuselage of B-17 (42-31889) was being flipped over on its back. Cables were attached to the nose section and a truck was used to pull the bomber over. (Franz Schraner)

With the bomber on its back, crews could easily remove the landing gear, wheels and other items. This was the normal procedure for American bombers which were scrapped in Switzerland after the war. The scrap metal was given to private industry. (Swissair)

All of the B-17 and B-24 fuselages dismantled and stored during the war were scrapped at Kloten and the metal was sold to local scrap yards where it was melted down. (Fotohaus Wiesner)

The storage depot of B-17 fuselages at Kloten. The wings were cut into two sections and stored separate from the fuselage. The USAAF decided that it was not worth the trouble of reassembling these aircraft and scrapped them in Switzerland. (Fotohaus Wiesener)

Between 27 August and 22 October 1945, a total of seventy-two aircraft were flown to Burtonwood; thirty B-17s, forty-one B-24s and the only flyable P-51. Some of the bombers that had been repaired and were intended to be flown out were not accepted by the Technical Commission. These aircraft were scrapped in Switzerland.

There was a considerable amount of other items from the interned bombers and airmen which had to be taken out of the country. Aircraft equipment (including bombs), flight suits and other items were transported out of the country in six large trucks, each carrying about twenty tons. Most was burned after it arrived at Munich-Erding.

Some of the equipment carried in the bombers was of interest to the Swiss. All rubber items (tires, tanks and so on) were kept in Switzerland. Additionally, all of the aluminum and steel scrap was highly appreciated by Swiss industry and, up to 6 December 1945, some 345 tons of aircraft scrap was given to private enterprises for their use. Half a million rounds of .50 caliber machine gun ammunition was taken to the *Munitionsfabrik* (ammunition plant) at Altdorf, where the ammunition was destroyed under American supervision. The gunpowder, lead and brass from the shells were used by the Swiss Army.

Ironically, the B-17s and B-24s which were flown to Burtonwood did not survive much longer than the bombers that were scrapped in Switzerland. These aircraft, maintained over months during their time in Switzerland, arrived too late to be flown from England back to the U.S. and it was decided to scrap them all at Burtonwood.

The bureaucratic "tug of war" between the U.S. and Swiss governments continued long after the last American bombers were scrapped. At the end of the war, the Swiss presented the USAAF with an invoice amounting to 4,964,992.00 Swiss Francs. This figure included the lodging of the interned airmen and the maintenance on the American aircraft during their stay in Switzerland. The settlement of this account dragged out over a two year period before a settlement of 4,520,000.00 Swiss Francs ($104,000.00) was agreed upon.

American engineers inspect engines at Dübendorf. These repairs and inspections had to be done carefully since the small field did not allow for test flights of the interned bombers. (Swissair)

USAAF ground crews leave a C-47 (42-93690) at Dübendorf. These men arrived in Switzerland to assist the Swiss in returning the interned bombers to a flyable condition so they could be flown out to England. (Franz Schraner)

This B-24G-16-NT (42-78458) is leaving Dübendorf for England with a replacement number one engine taken from an Olive Drab Liberator. The aircraft flew out on 22 September 1945. (A. Muser)

The Swiss had indicated their desire that GEN LeMay, Commanding General of the United States Air Forces in Europe, make the presentation of the check to the Swiss Government. This was agreeable with GEN LeMay and on 22 December 1947, GEN LeMay and COL W.B. Mann departed for Switzerland. Bad weather kept them from landing and on two successive attempts, the trip was cancelled for one reason or another. Finally BGEN Schneider, representing GEN LeMay (who was unable to make the trip), accompanied COL W.B. Mann to Switzerland and made the presentation on 26 January 1948, fulfilling the U.S. obligation to Switzerland.

Transport aircraft and interned bombers are lined up at Burtonwood, England, after they had been flown from Dübendorf to England. The engine is from the B-17G-5-DL (42-3524) *Vonnie Gal* and the tail of the Natural Metal Flying Fortress belongs to *HELL'S BELLE*. (Logan Muster)